The African-American Male

The African-American Male

An Annotated Bibliography

Compiled by
JACOB U. GORDON

Bibliographies and Indexes in Afro-American and African Studies,
Number 39

Greenwood Press
Westport, Connecticut • London

Library of Congress Cataloging-in-Publication Data

Gordon, Jacob U.
    The African-American male : an annotated bibliography /
compiled by Jacob U. Gordon.
        p.   cm.—(Bibliographies and indexes in Afro-American and
    African studies, ISSN 0742–6925 ; no. 39)
        Includes indexes.
        ISBN 0–313–30656–7 (alk. paper)
        1. Afro-American men Bibliography.   2. Afro-American boys
    Bibliography.   I. Title.   II. Series.
    Z1361.N39G67   1999
    [E185.86]
    016.30538'896073—dc21   99–21785

British Library Cataloguing in Publication Data is available.

Library of Congress Catalog Card Number: 99–21785
ISBN: 0–313–30656–7
ISSN: 0742–6925

First published in 1999

Greenwood Press, 88 Post Road West, Westport, CT 06881
An imprint of Greenwood Publishing Group, Inc.
www.greenwood.com

Printed in the United States of America

The paper used in this book complies with the
Permanent Paper Standard issued by the National
Information Standards Organization (Z39.48–1984).

10 9 8 7 6 5 4 3 2 1

Contents

Acknowledgments

Virtually every book is a product of many different contributions. This volume is no exception. I owe a special debt to my staff, especially Bridgitt Mitchell, at the Center for Multicultural Leadership Research, and my colleagues in the Department of African and African American Studies at the University of Kansas. I am particularly grateful to my students in my undergraduate University Honors, Civil Rights Movement, and Black Leadership classes. Under the supervision of my graduate research assistant, Katie Woods of the History Department, these students played a major role in collecting and reviewing hundreds of works on African-American men and boys.

To all of those connected with the African-American Men and Boys Initiative at the W.K. Kellogg Foundation, The Village Foundation, the Jane Addams Hull House Association and the National African-American Male Collaboration, and especially Dr. Bobby Austin, I am eternally grateful. Without these resources this book wouldn't have been possible. To Dr. Bobby Austin, whose vision created the national initiative on African-American Men and Boys, I gladly dedicate this book.

Finally, and most important, I owe my greatest debt of thanks to Katie Woods, my graduate research assistant, for her tireless efforts toward making this book a reality.

Introduction

The plight of African-American men and boys in America has been well documented by researchers and practitioners: Wilkinson and Taylor, 1977; Gibbs, 1988; Gordon and Majors, 1994; and Austin, 1996 to name a few.

A recent publication, *Repairing the Breach* (Austin, 1996), provides another alarming data on the status of African-American men and boys. A National Task Force Report under the sponsorship of the W.K. Kellogg Foundation, among other things, has concluded:

African-American males (and the larger African-American community) have faced continuous forms of mistreatment and oppression. The denial of the opportunity to vote, the denial of higher-paying industrial jobs, the denial of educational opportunities, and other related forms of racial discrimination all reflected practices and policies deeply rooted in American thought and American traditions. And the consequences of these historical practices are still very much with us today.

Other sources of research data confirm the conclusion of the Task Force as they reveal the following statistical overview of the status of African-American men and boys:

Population
- Total U.S. population is 248,709,873. The total African-American population is 29,930,524 (12%). Of this number,

14,170,151 are males; Black males represent 6% of the U.S. population (U.S. Census, 1990).

Health

- Black male life expectancy in 1991 is 64.6. White male life expectancy in 1991 is 72.9.
- Black male death rates for HIV in 1991 is 52.9. White male death rates for HIV in 1991 is 16.7 (National Center for Health Statistics, 1994).
- Black males are more likely to be born to unwed teenage mothers who themselves have limited education and even more limited life choices (Gibbs, 1988).

Homicide

- Homicide rates in 1991 for African-American males were 72.5 per 100,000, nearly 8 times higher than for White males. (FBI, 1993).

Poverty

- The rate of poverty for all African-Americans is 29.5% compared to a 9.8% for Whites (U.S. Census, 1992).
- Nearly half (42.7%) of Black youth under 18 live in families below the poverty line (Curtis, 1996).

Family Life

- Of the 7,055,063 Black families, Black females head 3,045,283 (43%). 26.3% of all Black families live in poverty, compared to 7.0% of White families (U.S. Census, 1992).

Incarceration

- Almost one in three (33%) Black males between the ages of 20 and 29 is under the control of the criminal justice system-- in prison, jail, on probation, or on parole. This compares with one in sixteen White males and one in ten Hispanic males (Maurer, 1990).
- The number of African-American males in prison and jail exceeds the number of African-American males enrolled in higher education; 3% in higher education and nearly 50% in the criminal justice system (Maurer, 1990).
- Black men in the United States are imprisoned at a rate four times that of Black men in South Africa: 3,109 per 100,000 compared to 729 per 100,000 (Morton and Snell, 1992).
- Forty-four percent of all prisoners in the United States are Black; Black men make up 40% of the condemned on death row (Sentencing Project, 1990).

Education

- More than 20% of the Black male adolescents in the 12-17 age groups were unable to read at the 4th grade level (Brown, 1979).

Stereotypes

- The Black male has been negatively portrayed in the media and the literature more than any other group in American history (Drake and Cayton, 1945; Gibbs, 1988).

Jobs

- Unemployment among Black youth was 34%--twice the rate of all teenagers, 17.4% (Gibbs, 1988).

By most demographic indices--mortality, health, crime, homicide, life expectancy, income, education, unemployment, and marital status--African-American men have the smallest chance to achieve the American dream. In fact, of the four comparison groups (Black males, Black females, White males, White females), social indicators show that Black males experience the highest rates of health and social problems, including heart disease, hypertension, diabetes, homicide, suicide, unemployment, delinquency and crime, school dropout, imprisonment, and unwed teenage parenthood (Gordon and Majors, 1994). As Gibbs (1988) put it, Black males have been miseducated by the educational system, mishandled by the criminal justice system, mislabeled by the mental health system, and misread by the social welfare system. In fact, she argues that Black males have become rejects of the American affluent society and misfits in their own communities.

The men's studies movement is a relatively new phenomenon in the American academic community. However, there have been, for some time, different areas of interest about men's life which have attracted scholars. For example, many psychiatrists have been interested in men's behavior, the notion of masculinity, the lives of great men, etc. Moreover, the recent women's studies movement has spawned both activist and scholarly interests in men's studies. Journals of African-American Men were established in the 1990s. What continues to be lacking however, is the paucity of basic reference materials for men's studies. This is particularly a major problem for the study of men of color.

The only annotated bibliographic work on Black American men was commissioned by the American Psychological Association (APA) in 1987. Brenda Evans and James Whitfield completed their work on the Black male in 1988. The book, which was entitled *Black Males in the United States: An Annotated Bibliography*, was a compilation of psychological studies on Black men drawn from journal articles and dissertations. The materials covered the period from 1967 to 1987. The present volume fills a major part of the existing gap in Black male studies. Unlike the only previous work in this field, this publication is comprehensive. It is multidisciplinary, covering a wide range of subjects. Yet it should be noted that the book was not intended to be exhaustive.

One of the most troubled segments of our society is the African-American male. The statistics on the African-American male population make it imperative to develop a deeper knowledge and understanding of this group. America will experience a great human loss if the current trend remains unchecked. It is hypothesized that a deeper understanding of the African-American male is sin qua non to any effective measures that will ameliorate the present condition. This annotated bibliography is, I believe, an important factor in deepening our academic and effective domains of Black male studies. The publication is useful as a reference tool to libraries, human service agencies, government officials and researchers, especially in gender studies and Black studies.

More than nine hundred sources have been organized in this book by subject areas including education, health, crime, civil rights, leadership, sports, entertainment and history. The document includes books, articles, chapters, and monographs. A non-indexed compilation of doctoral dissertations is also included.

Regrettably, it was not possible to provide annotations for all the materials included in this book. Indeed such an effort would have been futile. Some of the materials were not available for our review at the completion of this work. However, because they were central to the concern of this book, they have been listed with full citations as selected works on the African-American male.

This book is the product of a national project initiated by the W.K. Kellogg Foundation. In September of 1993, the W.K. Kellogg Foundation launched the African-American Men and Boys (AAMB) initiative under the guidance of Dr. Bobby Austin to address some of the challenges facing this group of males. The first stage of the initiative included 13 programmatic projects and 2 technical projects. The second stage provided for an additional 17 projects to create model collaborations that could bring about long-term structural interventions at the community level.

Three principles have guided this initiative:

1.   Use leadership development, capacity-building and skills-building to strengthen the leaders of the 13 new or expanded programs;

2. Develop a model, free-standing collaboration for projects to capitalize on each other's strengths and provide more resources and services than they would on their own and, ultimately, achieve ways of sustaining themselves; and

3. Find additional successful projects, develop criteria for establishing models for replication and focus on structures for leveraging funds that will lead to long-term sustainability and systems change.

The AAMB initiative strives to provide communities with a wide array of effective programs and resources to meet the needs of young men--not merely a focused drug prevention or anti-violence program. While many of the programs focus on a particular program or service, most include a wide array of opportunities for their participants. The strength of the AAMB initiative is the linking together of programs to form a network to learn from each other, share resources and expertise to strengthen and expand their own programs. By doing so, they can all offer more holistic, comprehensive services to meet the needs of African-American males and to address complex interconnected problems in their communities.

From the spirit of the AAMB initiative grew the National African-American Male Collaboration in the summer of 1995. This model collaboration has demonstrated the whole is truly greater than the sum of its parts. Each participating agency now has the capacity and ability to draw on services, expertise and other great resources from all the other projects in the collaboration.

The National African-American Male Collaboration forms a network of support, resources, talents and research to achieve a common purpose: *improving the quality of life for African-American males, developing healthy minds and bodies and building leadership skills in youth.*

The Jane Addams Hull House Association in Chicago serves as secretariat of the Collaboration. As secretariat, Hull House Association is responsible for coordinating the National African-American Male Collaboration and individually working with member agencies to enhance their capabilities.

In designing and implementing methods to strengthen and enhance the participating agencies, Hull House Association recognizes three critical and interdependent aspects of organizational development:

1. Training
2. Resource Development
3. Networking

Since its founding in 1889 by Jane Addams, Hull House Association has worked in Chicago's communities, helping people to help themselves. Comprised of over 100 strength-based programs that encourage self-reliance, Hull House Association serves over 225,000 annually. Hull House Association programs encompass childcare, child welfare services, family support education, recreation, senior services and economic development.

At the time of completing this volume, the W.K. Kellogg Foundation Initiative had been transferred to the Village Foundation in the Washington D.C. area. Dr. Bobby Austin, formerly of the Kellogg Foundation, now serves as the President and CEO of the Village Foundation. The former American Ambassador to the United Nations, the Honorable Andrew Young serves as the Chair of the Board of Directors of the Village Foundation. The mission and vision of the Village Foundation is an outgrowth of recommendations by the National Advisory Task Force on African-American Men and Boys led by Ambassador Andrew Young and sponsored by the W.K. Kellogg Foundation. The groundwork for the Foundation is based on the Task Force's 1996 report, "Repairing the Breach: Key Ways to Support Family Life, Reclaim our Streets, and Rebuild Civil Society in America's Communities" (Alpine Guild, Inc., 1996).

1

General

001. Austin, Lettie J. and Nelson, Sophia P. (eds.). *The Black Man and the Promise of America*. Chicago: Scott, Foresman, & Co., 1970. 523 pp., includes index and bibliography. ISBN 0-673-05675-9. This book addresses the ability to make the American dream a reality for all. It takes a historical and literary perspective on Black and White interactions and relationships. The book is divided into four parts: documenting the slave trade, evidence of Black attempts to achieve true citizenship and the thwarting of these endeavors, social picture of the distorted personality that comes from separate environments for Whites and Blacks, and a focus on Black contributions to American culture.

002. Baker, Houston A. *Black Studies, Rap, and the Academy*. Chicago: University of Chicago Press, 1993. 110 pp., includes index, hardcover $16.95, paperback $9.95. ISBN 0-226-03520-4 (H), 0-226-03521-2 (P). Baker begins with the origins of Black Studies, which has come to define the state of race relations in America. Specific case studies are presented within the rap realm as he offers a celebratory analysis of rap's techniques, strategies, and unique creativity. Additionally, Baker presents a mediation on the academy and Black urban living. The book shows concern for the future of the American academy and American race relations and the balancing of controversies.

003. Booker, Simeon S. *Black Men's America*. Englewood Cliffs, NJ:
      Prentice Hall, 1964. 230 pp. Simeon gives us an account of some of his
      life experiences in this book. He tells about his experiences with
      Eisenhower and Richard Nixon. He also gives the reader insight into the
      attributes and attitudes of civil rights leaders of the 1960s, with whom he
      was acquainted.

004. Brown, William Wells. *The Black Man: His Antecedents, His Genius,
      and His Achievements*. New York: Kraus Reprint Co., 1969. 312 pp.
      Brown gives well-written accounts of more than 50 Black men and
      women from 1969 and before. He highlights their talents, achievements,
      and devotion to the welfare of their race. The subjects of these
      biographies exhibit the versatility and range of the genius of African-
      Americans.

005. Cohen, David and Collins, Charles (eds.). *The African-Americans*. New
      York: Penguin Books Publishing, 1994. 240 pp., includes bibliography
      and index, hardcover $45.00. ISBN 0-670-84982-0. Cohen and Collins
      provide an inside look at the African-American. Political leaders, as well
      as unsung heroes' lives are depicted in more than 200 photographs with
      honest captions. The editors give detailed descriptions of subjects'
      activities, hardships, and accomplishments. The book explores both the
      diversity and the positive aspects of the 20th century African-American.

006. Finkelman, Paul (ed.). *African-Americans and the Legal Profession in
      Historical Perspective*. New York: Garland, 1992. 529 pp., includes
      bibliography.   ISBN 0-815-30543-5.   This book discusses the
      participation of Blacks in law. One section discusses court cases such as
      Dred Scot v. Sanford and *Brown v. Board of Education*. The Black Bar
      Association, Black Lawyers, education and community, and Black Law
      Schools are discussed in the latter parts of the book.

007. Frazier, Edward Franklin. *Black Bourgeoisie*. New York: Free Press
      Paperbacks, 1997. 264 pp., includes index and bibliography, paperback
      $12.00.   ISBN 0-684-83241-0.   Frazier discusses the diversity and
      complexity in political discourse, family, and community of middle-class
      Blacks. He also discusses the future of Blacks regarding racial equality
      while analyzing the Black middle-class and economy. Throughout the
      book he encourages middle-class Blacks to remain loyal to their cultural
      and social obligations.

008. Gates, Henry Louis Jr. and West, Cornel. *The Future of the Race*. New
      York: Alfred A. Knopf, Inc., 1996. 196 pp., includes bibliography,

hardcover $21.00, paperback $12.00. ISBN 0-679-44405-X (H), 0-679-76378-3 (P). This is an attempt by Gates and West to reexamine W.E.B. DuBois' philosophies and beliefs and to place his ideas in a contemporary context. Gates uses this opportunity to respond to DuBois in the form of an autobiographical account of the triumphs and tragedies of the generation of young Blacks who first attended historically all-White institutions such as Yale University, where he was an undergraduate. He also examines the paradox of a growing Black middle-class coexisting with a growing Black lower-class. The second half of this book is West's essay investigating DuBois' life as a thinker and particularly his political and philosophical ideas. West situates DuBois in the context of his times and within the limitations imposed by social, intellectual, and political constraints.

009. Gordon, Jacob U. and Majors, Richard (eds.). *The American Black Male: His Present Status and His Future.* Chicago: Nelson Hall, 1994. 315 pp., paperback $21.95. ISBN 0-830-41236-0. Psychologist Majors and historian Gordon, founders of the National Council of African-American Men (NCAAM), have put together a collection of 21 articles examining the Black American male's condition within the context of a society that has stereotyped and marginalized the Black male in every official index. The essays, by various contributors, cover such topics as health, AIDS, poverty, unemployment, family life, violence, substance abuse, the criminal justice system, homelessness, racism, gender relations, mental health and men's studies. In his conclusion Majors puts forward a case for all-Black schools with Africanized curriculums. This is an important book for those involved in public policy, social science, government, education, social work, justice officials and political, civil rights, business, and civil leaders will read this book as well as those using it as a text book for course work.

010. Hamilton, James B. *What a Time to Live: The Autobiography of James B. Hamilton.* East Lansing, Michigan: Michigan State University, 1995. 194 pp., includes bibliography, hardcover $22.95. ISBN 0-870-13353-5. Hamilton is a very successful African-American chemist and administrator at Michigan State University. In this autobiography, he focuses on his 25-year career at MSU. He also describes his childhood, the path that led him to his success, and the obstacles he encountered along the way. The book gives a powerful description of what it took for African-Americans to succeed in the past, as well as the present.

011. Hutchinson, Earl O. *Beyond O.J.: Race, Sex, and Class Lessons for America.* Los Angeles, CA: Middle Passage Press, 1996. 200 pp.,

hardcover $50.00, paperback $19.95. ISBN 1-551-64050-1 (H), 1-551-64050-3 (P). Hutchinson was a Simpson trial analyst for the CBS-TV affiliate in Los Angeles and writes a book about the Simpson experience and the issues surrounding it. He is not interested in explosive revelations, but rather concerns himself with what the O.J. case made America realize about itself. Among other things, Hutchinson explores the taboos of interracial marriage, America's obsession with stereotyping race, class and sex, the need to make icons out of sporting heroes, the playing of the race card, and racial conspiracy theories. Hutchinson concludes by exposing the deep racial and class double standards in the criminal justice system and how America has made crime and punishment a racial problem, not an American problem.

012. Johnson, Charles and McCluskey, John, Jr. (eds.). *Black Men Speaking*. Bloomington: Indiana University Press, 1997.   208 pp., includes bibliography, hardcover $24.95. ISBN 0-253-33259-1. Divided into 10 sections, this book gives voice to the Black man in America. Combining interviews, poems, and other sources, the editors challenge stereotypes of Black men as they explore education, music, discipline, and a number of other areas. A telling essay explores what it feels like to be a problem in society from the perspective of a Black man.

013. Miedzian, Myriam. *Boys Will Be Boys: Breaking the Link Between Masculinity and Violence*. New York: Anchor Books, 1991. 354 pp., paperback $14.00. ISBN 0-385-42254-7. Miedzian, a philosophy professor, argues that society's portrayal of the "Masculine Mystique" perpetuates male violence and aggression in the early years of a boy's life. Based on extensive research, she argues that aggressive behavior can be curbed by teaching nonviolent resolution in schools and encouraging boys to bond with babies when they are young.

014. Powell, Kevin and Baraka, Ras (eds.). *In the Tradition: An Anthology of Young Black Writers*. New York: Harlem Press, 1992.   398 pp., hardcover $28.00, paperback $14.00. ISBN 0-863-16315-7 (H), 0-863-16316-5 (P). This is a well-crafted collection of poetry and fiction. The works articulate the experience of African-Americans and others in the Diaspora. Among other subjects, the contributors address hip-hop music, politics, ancestors, and the middle passage.

015. Smith, J. Clay. *Emancipation: The Making of the Black Lawyer, 1844-1944*. Philadelphia: University of Pennsylvania Press, 1993.   703 pp., includes index and bibliography, hardcover $56.95. ISBN 1-812-23181-3. Smith provides an account of the first African-American lawyers and

their experience of desegregating a traditionally White profession. He offers information pertaining to all Black lawyers as he tells the story of these men's work, which in turn aided the civil rights legislation of the twentieth century. Smith focuses on the individual, state, and national levels as well as legal groups and organizations. Also included in the study are accounts of individual lawyers.

016. Stein, Judith. *The World of Marcus Garvey: Race and Class in Modern Society.* Baton Rouge: Louisiana State University, 1986. 294 pp., includes index and bibliography, paperback $14.95. ISBN 0-807-11670-X. Stein takes an in-depth look at Marcus Garvey and his crusade for Black Nationalism. She details the actions of Garvey in the Universal Negro Improvement Association (UNIA) and while at the helm of the Black Star Line.

017. Teague, Bob. *Letters to a Black Boy.* New York: Walker, 1968. 211 pp. ISBN 0-802-70167-1. Bob Teague, a Newscaster for NBC-TV in 1968, writes a series of letters to his son, aged two at the time, to be read when he reaches the age of thirteen. *Letters to a Black Boy* is an attempt by Teague to prepare his son for the problems of being Black in a White society. His letters are often as humorous as they are angry. They contain a message for Whites and Blacks alike on living in what he sees as an inherently racist society.

018. Wilkinson, Doris Y. and Taylor, Ronald. *The Black Male in America: Perspectives on His Status in Contemporary Society.* Chicago, IL: Nelson-Hall, 1977. 375 pp., includes index and bibliography, hardcover $38.95. ISBN 0-882-29227-7. Taylor and Wilkinson take a look at the misrepresentation of Black males in society. They deal with the falsehoods of Black males in the cultural, economic, and political arenas. They prove that the stereotypical Moynihan report contradicts what the Black male stands for in society. The authors put together a collection of essays by professional academics that denounce stereotypes and focus on reality.

019. Woodson, Carter G. *The Negro Professional Man and the Community with Special Emphasis on the Physician and the Lawyer.* Washington, DC: The Association for the Study of Negro Life and History, 1971. 155 pp., $29.95. ISBN 0-384-69208-7. Woodson provides an in-depth analysis of Black intellectual men as agents for community change and sweeping social transformations. At a time when life was hard for everyone in America, it was inestimably more so for Blacks and thus he sought to empower the Black community through education. His research

attempted to debunk the racist attitudes of White scholars toward African-Americans. He shifted the attention away from viewing Blacks solely as victims of American history, but rather as major actors.

020. Wright, Bruce. *Black Robes, White Justice.* Secaucus, NJ: Lyle Stuart, 1987. Paperback $15.95. ISBN 0-818-40422-1 (H), 0-818-40573-2 (P). A controversial New York City judge, Bruce Wright presents an attack on the criminal court system that is intended to infuriate his opposition. His major contention is that, in a system where most judges are White and most defendants are Black, judges are "ignorant of and indifferent to the debased reality of those who are judged." The book offers various accounts of painful racial episodes that he has experienced or observed in the courtroom and elsewhere. Topics range from relations between Blacks and Jews, to conflicts with New York City police over his lenient bail policies. Wright ultimately suggests that better education of potential judges in racial aspects of U.S. history might improve the situation.

2

Arts and Entertainment

021. Abdul, Raoul. *Famous Black Entertainers of Today.* New York: Dodd, Mead & Company, 1974. 159 pp., includes index. ISBN 0-396-06849-9. Abdul writes in-depth profiles of eighteen leading Black figures in the entertainment industry. Some of the people he writes about are actor James Earl Jones and Broadway actor Ben Vereen. He conducted interviews with the entertainers, as well as those close to them. The profiles trace not only their entertainment careers, but often their childhoods as well. Abdul also writes about the emergence of Blacks in all facets of entertainment, and how that emergence has helped shatter stereotypes.

022. Bogle, Donald. *Blacks in American Films and Television: An Encyclopedia.* New York: Garland Publishers, 1988. 510 pp., includes index and bibliography, $60.00. ISBN 0-824-08715-1. In this three-part encyclopedia divided into Movies, Television, and Profiles, Bogle researches the development of the portrayal of Blacks in entertainment. After each segment there is a summary and critique as well as a list of directors, stars, and producers. The profiles consist of a chronology of their careers and birth/death dates.

023. Boskin, Joseph. *Sambo: The Rise and Demise of an American Jester.* New York: Oxford University Press, 1986. 252 pp., includes index and bibliography, $20.95. ISBN 0-195-05658-2. Boskin presents the five

traditional Black Sambo positions: plantation darky, joke subject, postcard joke, chauffeur and minstrel. He examines Sambo's roots in slavery and the plantation system, and rejects Black actors, such as Eddie Anderson from the Jack Benny Show, who perpetuated this image.

024. Carroll, Rebecca (ed.). *Swing Low: Black Men Writing*. New York: Carol Southern Books, 1995. 266 pp., paperback $9.60. ISBN 0-517-88324-4. John Edgar Wideman, Leon Forrest, Henry Louis Gates, Jr., Trey Ellis, Ishmael Reed, Nathan McCall, August Wilson, Cecil Brown, Wesley Brown, Cornelius Eady, Charles Johnson, Yusef Komunyakaa, Caryl Phillips, Darryl Pinckney, Greg Tate, and David Bradley--any collection with so many great writers is worth serious consideration. Carroll interviews the 16 authors, provides a full-page photo and short biography of each, and includes excerpts from their familiar works in fiction, poetry, and nonfiction.

025. Costello, Mark and Wallace, David Foster. *Signifying Rappers: Rap and Race in the Urban Present*. New York: Ecco Press, 1990. 140 pp., includes bibliography, paperback $11.00. ISBN 0-880-01535-7. Based primarily on the authors' experiences hanging out with the owners of a small rap music production company, the first part of this long essay on understanding rap describes the setting in which this music has arisen--the urban ghetto, in this case, the North Dorchester section of Boston. We get a vivid picture of rap's real-life context in an area of poverty and drugs, an environment mostly unknown to upscale Whites. Much of the book is devoted to a critical explication and validation of rap, including literary and historical analysis, placing it for instance in the context of African oral tradition.

026. Cripps, Thomas. *Slow Fade to Black: The Negro in American Film, 1900-1942*. New York: Oxford University Press, 1993. 447 pp., includes bibliography and index. ISBN 0-195-02130-4. Cripps records the role and depiction of African-Americans in film through World War II. He analyzes films such as D.W. Griffith's "Birth of a Nation" as he explores the evolution of racial attitudes in society as well as in film.

027. Cross, Brian. *It's Not About a Salary . . . Rap, Race and Resistance in Los Angeles*. New York: Verso Books, 1994. 304 pp., paperback $17.95. ISBN 0-860-91445-3. Cross takes his title from "Gangsta Gangsta," the classic rap by the group NWA, in which a refrain couplet claims: "It's not about a salary / It's all about reality." He provides a knowledgeable and detailed history of the idiom, going back to Slim Gaillard and beyond, to the nations of West Africa. He also provides an extensive collection of

primary sources in his interviews with pioneers of the Los Angeles rap scene as well as hiphop's established aristocrats.

028. Delaney, Beauford. *Beauford Delaney, A Retrospective.* New York: The Studio Museum in Harlem, 1978. Includes an index. ISBN 9-993-77825-7. Delaney was considered the "dean of American Negro painters living abroad." This autobiography details the development of his art, his education and tutoring, his experiences abroad, and his artistic style.

029. Gill, Glenda E. *White Grease Paint on Black Performers: A Study of the Federal Theatre Project 1935-1939.* New York: Peter Lang Publishing Inc., 1988. 220 pp., includes bibliography, $36.00. Gill examines the impact of the FTP on the lives of 7 members of the New York City "Negro" units. A chapter is devoted to each actor, detailing their connection to the FTP, and telling about the rest of their careers. Canada Lee, Rex Ingram, Edna Thomas, Thomas Anderson, Arthur "Dooley" Wilson, Dick Campbell, and Leonard de Paur are the seven Black actors and actresses Gill studies.

030. Golden, Thelma. *Black Male: Representations of Masculinity in Contemporary American Art.* New York: Whitney Museum of American Art, 1994. 223 pp., includes bibliography and index. ISBN 0-810-96816-9. Golden is fascinated by racist depictions of Black people in American art. She provides here a view into her collection of racist images of Blacks, which now numbers around 10,000.

031. Handy, D. Antoinette. *Black Conductors.* Metuchen, NJ: The Scarecrow Press, Inc., 1995. 557 pp., includes bibliography and index, hardcover $69.50. ISBN 0-810-82930-4. A symphony musician, Handy put together a book that gives profiles of great Black conductors such as Count Basie and Duke Ellington. She includes all types of music such as musical theater and jazz. The book gives an overview of the Black conductors in each particular music genre.

032. Handy, William Christopher. *Negro Authors and Composers of the United States.* New York: AMS Press, 1976. 24 pp., includes bibliography, hardcover $27.50. ISBN 0-404-12953-6. W.C. Handy, an African-American author, provides a book on famous Black composers and authors. He covers greats such as Duke Ellington and Jimmy Cox. Along with biographical information, Handy includes verses from songs and titles of famous works.

033. Harper, Donna Sullivan. *Not so Simple: The "Simple" Stories by
      Langston Hughes*. Columbia, MO: University of Missouri Press, 1995.
      260 pp., includes bibliography and index, paperback $19.95. ISBN 0-
      826-21088-0. Harper describes the development of Langston Hughes's
      one great fictional character, Harlemite Jesse B. Simple.   Hughes
      introduced this sidewalk sage in a weekly column for the *Chicago
      Defender*. Simple went on to star in six books and a play. Harper, a
      professor at Spellman College, has written the definitive account of the
      birth and development of Jesse B. Simple. She also describes Hughes as
      he planned publishing strategies and negotiated with editors and agents.

034. Heath, Gordon. *Deep are the Roots: The Memoirs of a Black Expatriate*.
      Amherst: University of Massachusetts Press, 1992. 200 pp., includes
      bibliography and index, paperback $14.95. ISBN 1-558-49020-5. This
      strongly written memoir is a welcome addition to the literature of a sad
      chapter in American art. Heath (1918-1991) was a gay Black American
      actor. His deeply etched memories re-create a world of Black New York
      in the 1920s and 30s that is clear and passionate. Heath's family, friends,
      ideas, and influences of self are fully drawn. The title comes from his
      success as an actor on Broadway in Elia Kazan's "Deep are the Roots."

035. Hill, Errol. *Shakespeare in Sable: A History of Black Shakespearean
      Actors*. Amherst, MA: University of Massachusetts Press, 1986. 216 pp.,
      includes index, paperback $16.95. ISBN 0-870-23525-7. Beginning with
      the African Company in 1821, Hill describes the difficulties Black actors
      encountered in playing non-Black characters in Shakespeare's plays. He
      also describes successes of Black actors in these roles, including Ira
      Aldridge's performances in Europe and memorable productions by Black
      units of the Federal Theater Project.

036. Isaacs, Edith J.R. *The Negro in the American Theater*. New York:
      Theater Arts, 1947. 143 pp. This is a well-illustrated and well-written
      account of African-American composers, playwrights, and performers in
      American theater from the 1800s to 1947. The book contains portraits
      and scenes from outstanding plays featuring Black actors.   More
      specifically, this book explores Blacks' rise to accomplishment in the
      American theater throughout the past century.

037. Kirschke, Amy H. *Aaron Douglas: Art, Race, and the Harlem
      Renaissance*. Jackson: University Press of Mississippi, 1995. 166 pp.,
      includes index, hardcover $45.00, paperback $19.95. ISBN 0-878-05775-
      7 (H), 0-878-05800-1 (P). Kirschke provides a thorough biography of
      Aaron Douglas, considered a "pioneering Africanist" and the "father of

African-American art." Douglas, the son of a baker in Topeka, was a member of the middle class and was mostly self-educated. As a central figure in the Harlem Renaissance, he believed that the future of the "New Negro" lay in the hands of the artist.

038. Patterson, Lindsay. *Anthology of the Afro-American in the Theatre: A Critical Approach*. New York: Publishers Co., 1976. 306 pp., includes bibliography. ISBN 0-877-81205-5. Patterson's book is a collection of essays and critical works dealing with the history of Blacks in the American entertainment industry. Included in this book are discussions of the impact of Blacks in theater, film, radio, and drama. Inherent in many of the essays are reflections on the barriers and injustices that Black entertainers faced throughout this century.

039. Peterson, Bernard L., Jr. *Contemporary Black American Playwrights and Their Plays: A Biographical Directory and Dramatic Index*. Westport, CT: Greenwood Press, 1988. 661 pp., $75.00. ISBN 0-313-25190-8. In this comprehensive directory, Peterson includes biographical information on more than 700 Black playwrights who were alive in 1950.

040. Potter, Russell A. *Spectacular Vernaculars: Hip Hop and the Politics of Postmodernism*. Albany: State University of New York Press, 1995. 197 pp., includes bibliography and index. ISBN 0-791-42626-2. Potter, a teacher at Rhode Island College, examines hip-hop's cultural rebellion in terms of its specific implications for postmodern theory and practice, using the politics of reception as its primary rhetorical ground.

041. Reagon, Bernice Johnson (ed.). *We'll Understand it Better By and By: Pioneering African-American Gospel Composers*. Washington, DC: Smithsonian Institution Press, 1992. 384 pp., includes bibliography and index, hardcover $24.95. ISBN 1-560-98167-9. This book brings together pioneering composers in gospel music and analyzes the evolution of their music as it shows the impact that gospel music has had on worship traditions and contemporary music. It gives an overview of gospel music and describes the migrations to urban settings, then focuses on six important figures in the history of gospel music. These include Charles Albert Tindley, Thomas A. Dorsey, William H. Brewster, Sr., and Kenneth Morris.

042. Ro, Ronin. *Merchandizing the Rhymes of Violence*. New York: St. Martin's Press, 1996. 192 pp., paperback $19.95. ISBN 0-312-14344-3. Ro, a freelance music reporter, provides a collection of his articles that trace rap music from 1992-1995, primarily in Los Angeles and New York

City. He argues that exploitative record companies and gangsta rappers have perverted and distorted hip-hop music. Once a unifying positive musical form, hip-hop has been packaged with gang-culture images and language with lyrics that promote violence, antisocial attitudes, misogyny, self-hatred, and murder. Ro profiles Method Man, NWA's Dr. Dre, Kid Frost, and other rappers.

043. Schiffman, Jack. *Harlem Heyday: A Pictorial History of Modern Black Show Business and the Apollo Theatre*. Buffalo, NY: Prometheus Books, 1984. 272 pp., includes index. ISBN 0-879-75247-5. Schiffman is an extraordinary writer who wrote a great deal about his own life experiences. He was introduced to theater and art at a relatively early age by his father, and his childhood memories surround the Apollo Theater. His father purchased the theater in 1935. Schiffman notes that every Black entertainer in modern history made his way across the stage of the Apollo Theater.

044. Schwartzman, Myron. *Romare Bearden: His Life and Art*. New York: H.N. Abrams, 1990. 320 pp., includes bibliography and index. ISBN 0-810-93108-7. In the 1940s, Bearden worked for the Department of Social Services. While working, he did art on the side and really lived his life through his art. He had a very large fan club, and a lot of his work was shown at the Cordice and Ekstrom Gallery.

045. Simmons, Renee Antoinette. *Frederick Douglass O'Neal: Pioneer of the Actors' Equity Association*. New York: Garland Publishing, Inc., 1996. 162 pp., includes bibliography and index. ISBN 0-815-32372-7. Simmons provides a complete biography of O'Neal. He was a pioneering actor, theater organizer, and union spokesman. In 1961 he was voted Vice President of the Actors' Equity Association, and in 1964 he was voted President, and served for nine years. O'Neal finally stepped down after a 60-year career and was voted to the 20th Century American Theatre Hall of Fame.

046. Smith, Eric Ledell. *Bert Williams: A Biography of the Pioneer Black Comedian*. Jefferson, NC: McFarland & Co., 1992. 301 pp., includes bibliography and index, hardcover $37.50. ISBN 0-899-50695-X. A book about the life and work of Bert Williams, this book spans his career in the show business industry from 1893-1922. He was a vaudeville and musical comedian and participated in the Ziegfeld Follies. Collaborations from longtime partner George Walker and other professional colleagues add to this biographical work.

047. Vega. *Into the Light, Out of the Darkness: The Art of the Black Male.* New York: Vega Press, 1996. 97 pp., paperback $30.00. ISBN 1-880-72914-8. This is a collection of photographs of Black male images. Poet Vega refers to his photographs as nudes, though the men do not show full frontal nudity. Vega writes that he attempts to define the subjects as "total spiritual, sensual, and cultural human beings." He is trying to counter the misrepresentation and lack of appreciation of Black male representations in popular cultural imagery.

048. Woll, Allen. *Black Musical Theatre: From* Coontown *to* Dreamgirls. Baton Rouge: Louisiana State University Press, 1989. 301 pp., hardcover $29.95, paperback $13.95. ISBN 0-807-11469-3 (H), 0-306-80454-9 (P). Woll provides a comprehensive listing of every major Black musical or revue from 1898 into the 1980s. He evaluates music critics, theater archives and playbills to highlight the political, social, and economic influences on theatre. Woll also traces stereotypes of Blacks on stage throughout the period in study. He provides information about composers, performing artists, librettists, lyricists, and producers.

3

Civil Rights

049. Balagoon, Kuwasi, et.al. *Look for Me in the Whirlwind: The Collective Autobiography of the New York 21*. New York: Random House, 1971. 364 pp., hardcover $18.95. ISBN 0-394-45343-3. Balagoon represents many of the defendants of the New York Panther trial in this book. These accounts give voice to men and women raised in the urban core. Issues addressed include the rise of Black Nationalism and Black self-awareness.

050. Bontemps, Arna Wendell. *Free at Last: The Life of Frederick Douglass*. New York: Dodd & Mead, 1971. 310 pp., includes index. ISBN 0-396-06308-X. Bontemps' biography of Frederick Douglass (1817-1895) is detailed and well researched. Among her sources are Douglass's personal papers. She details his family history and early years as well as his life as a significant Black leader.

051. Breitman, George (ed.). *Malcolm X Speaks: Selected Speeches and Statements*. New York: Grove Weidenfeld, 1990. 223 pp., hardcover $17.95, paperback $9.95. IBSN 0-873-48546-7 (H), 0-802-13213-8 (P). Breitman's biography of Malcolm X presents seventeen speeches given between November 1963 and February 21, 1965, including the famous "The Bullet or the Ballot" speech delivered in Cleveland in 1964. The speeches offer powerful challenges to the Black community and are still relevant today.

052. Carson, Clayborne. *In Struggle: SNCC and the Black Awakening of the 1960s*. Cambridge: Harvard University Press, 1995. 317 pp., includes bibliography and index, paperback $17.50. IBSN 9-995-70312-2 (H), 0-674-44727-1 (P). This book talks about the SNCC (the Student Nonviolent Coordinating Committee) which emerged in the 1950s. The group was at the center of a movement that changed not only the nation but transformed its participants. The book examines the rapid rise and fall of this group, its ideologies and methods, and the evolution of its radical nature.

053. Carson, Clayborne and Gellen, David (eds.). *Malcolm X: The FBI File*. New York: Carroll and Graf Publishers, Inc., 1991. 504 pp., includes bibliography and index, hardcover $13.95, paperback $6.99. IBSN 0-881-84758-5 (H), 0-345-40009-7 (P). Carson gives an overview of the enormous FBI file on Malcolm X. The file was started in 1953 after Malcolm X was released from a Boston prison. Carson compares Malcolm X to other Black leaders and J. Edgar Hoover to define Malcolm X's place in African-American history.

054. Cheek, William and Cheek, Aimee Lee. *John Mercer Langston and the Fight for Black Freedom, 1829-65*. Urbana: University of Illinois Press, 1996. 478 pp., includes bibliography and index, $34.95. ISBN 0-252-06591-3. A biography of the abolitionist, politician, lawyer and educator Langston, this book provides an account of 19th century America and Langston's life as a free man in Ohio before 1865. As the first president of the Equal Rights League, Langston is an important figure in the civil rights movement. It also gives insight into the lives of 19th century African-Americans.

055. Clarke, John H. (ed.). *Malcolm X: The Man and His Times*. Trenton, NJ: Africa World Press, Inc., 1990. 360 pp., includes bibliography, hardcover $35.00, paperback $14.95. ISBN 0-865-43201-5. This anthology exhibits essays by international scholars and activists who either knew Malcolm X, or were impacted by his philosophies. By including Malcolm's speeches and writings, Clarke demonstrates his political and global impact as well as his dedication to Islam.

056. Cleaver, Eldridge. *Soul on Ice*. New York: Dell Publishing Group, 1992. 210 pp., includes bibliography. ISBN 0-440-21128-X. The prison memoirs of Eldridge Cleaver, former Black Panther activist, provide a poignant description of the Black experience during the Civil Rights era. This beautifully written book shocked and outraged readers when first released in the 1970s.

057. Cole, Thomas R. *No Color Is My Kind: The Life of Eldrewey Stearns and the Integration of Houston.* Austin, TX: University of Texas Press, 1997. 239 pp., includes bibliography and index, paperback $17.95. ISBN 0-292-71198-0 (P), 0-292-71197-2 (H). Cole provides a biography of Eldrewey Stearns, an older African-American who tells his life story. As a young boy growing up in segregated Texas and then as a young man who became a civil rights leader, Stearns takes you through Houston before, during and after Houston's desegregation movement of 1959-1963.

058. Cone, James H. *Martin & Malcolm and America: A Dream or a Nightmare.* Maryknoll, NY: Orbis Books, 1992. 358 pp., includes bibliography and index, paperback $16.00. ISBN 0-883-44824-6. Cone examines the divergent philosophies of Martin Luther King, Jr. and Malcolm X. He offers an analysis of the similarities and differences in their political and social actions. In his conclusion, Cone discusses the intersection of these philosophies before their deaths.

059. Cottman, Michael H. *Million Man March.* New York: Crown Publishing Group, 1995. Paperback $14.00. ISBN 0-517-88763-0. This is the first book published to commemorate the Million Man March, the largest gathering of African-American men in the United States. It offers insight into the cross section of participants, the path each took to the March, and what they hoped to find once they arrived.

060. Evers-Williams, Myrlie with Peters, William. *For Us, The Living.* New York: Doubleday, 1967. Medgar Evers' widow provides a biography of her husband. Evers, the child of sharecroppers, was later a field secretary for the NAACP. Evers-Williams details his work with the association, and the events leading to his assassination.

061. Foner, Philip Sheldon (ed.). *The Black Panthers Speak.* New York: Da Capo Press, Inc., 1995. 281 pp., includes bibliography, paperback $13.95. ISBN 0-306-80627-4. This compilation of writings and other historical documents on the Black Panther Party addresses the development and ideologies of the Party, including their positions on Black separatism and the power structure.

062. Haley, Alex and X, Malcolm. *The Autobiography of Malcolm X.* New York: Ballantine Books, 1992. 527 pp., includes bibliography. ISBN 0-345-37671-4. In collaboration with Alex Haley, Malcolm X reveals an insightful look into his journey from childhood through prison and into

the Nation of Islam. This powerful memoir documents a difficult era as it traces Malcolm X's rise to leadership during the Civil Rights Movement.

063.   Haywood, Harry. *Black Bolshevik: Autobiography of an Afro-American Communist.* Chicago: Liberator Press, 1978. 700 pp., includes bibliography, index and illustrations, paperback $15.00. ISBN 0-930-72052-0. This detailed memoir is an essential addition to any collection on Black radicalism and the Communist Party. One of the earliest Black recruits to the US Communist Party, Haywood followed his older brother into the Party in 1923. Haywood also discusses his role in the Communist Party International's strategy for Black liberation as the head of its Negro Department in the 1930s.

064.   Hilliard, David and Cole, Lewis. *This Side of Glory: The Autobiography of David Hilliard and the Story of the Black Panther Party.* Boston: Little Brown, 1993. 450 pp., includes index, hardcover $24.95, paperback $12.95. ISBN 0-316-36415-0 (H), 0-316-36421-5 (P). David Hilliard, chief of staff of the Black Panther Party, provides a telling history of the Party through his autobiography. Supplemented by stories shared by his Black and White associates as well as FBI materials, Hilliard's autobiography details the rise and fall of his childhood friend, Huey P. Newton, and the Black Panther Party.

065.   Kasher, Steven. *The Civil Rights Movement: A Photographic History, 1954-1968.* New York: Abbeville Publishing, 1996. 235 pp., includes bibliography and index, hardcover $35.00. ISBN 0-789-20123-2. With a foreword by the wife of slain Civil Rights activist Medgar Evers, Kasher captures the energy, struggle, and horror of the era. The candid and dramatic photographic coverage draws the reader into the confrontations of the Civil Rights Movement. Kasher covers the Freedom Summer, Montgomery Bus Boycott, and speeches and marches led by Malcolm X and Martin Luther King, Jr.

066.   Lewis, David Levering. *W.E.B. DuBois: A Biography of Race, 1868-1919.* New York: Henry Holt Co., Inc, 1997. 735 pp., includes bibliography and index, paperback $17.95. ISBN 0-805-03568-0. With 36 pages of family and friends' photographs, Lewis outlines DuBois' entire life. This 1994 Pulitzer-Prize winning biography gives a comprehensive inside view of the life of an American hero, activist, and educator.

067.   Lewis, Rupert. *Marcus Garvey: Anti-Colonial Champion.* Trenton, NJ: Africa World Press, Inc., 1988. 301 pp., includes bibliography and index,

paperback $11.95. ISBN 0-865-43061-6 (H), 0-865-43062-4 (P). An African-American scholar and author, Lewis examines Garvey's life and his fight against racism and colonialism. Lewis traces Garvey's life and work starting with his parentage and continuing through his political legacy. Garvey's theories on self-determination, the similarities of oppressed peoples, and the position of Blacks as an international problem, were at the heart of his push for decolonization.

068. Madhubuti, Haki R. and Karenga, Maulana. *Million Man March/A Day of Absence: A Commemorative Anthology: Speeches, Commentary, Photography, Poetry, Illustrations, and Documents.* Chicago: Third World Press, 1996. 172 pp., paperback $19.95. ISBN 0-883-78188-3. The Million Man March was a historic event for the African-American community. This anthology gives an itinerary of the day including speeches, photographs, and perspectives of the march from activist men and women. The editors include poems, tributes, and commentaries on the speeches.

069. Martin, Tony. *Marcus Garvey, Hero: A First Biography.* Dover, MA: The Majority Press, 1983. 179 pp., includes bibliography and index. ISBN 0-912-46904-8. An African-American author and historian, Martin's book is a brief account of Marcus Garvey's life. Incorporating the most current research on Garvey, Martin outlines not only his life but also his continuing impact. Martin also addresses the reasons behind Garvey's popularity.

070. McNeil, Genna R. *Groundwork: Charles Hamilton Houston and the Struggle for Civil Rights.* Philadelphia, PA: University of Pennsylvania Press, 1983. 224 pp., hardcover $27.50, paperback $20.95. ISBN 0-8122-7878-X (H), 0-81221-179-0 (P). This book is an exploration of the life of a prominent Civil Rights lawyer, Charles Hamilton Houston. McNeil's biography is a survey of Houston's accomplishments. His work was a precursor to the work of people like Martin Luther King, Jr. and Medgar Evers.

071. Mfume, Kweisi and Stodgill, R. *No Free Ride: From the Mean Streets to the Mainstream.* New York, NY: One World, 1996. 373 pp., hardcover $25.00, paperback $12.00. ISBN 0-34539-220-5. Kweisi Mfume, CEO of the NAACP and a former five-time congressman from Maryland, traces his life story from his early life in crime and poverty to his later religious awakening and involvement in politics. This is a vivid and detailed autobiography.

072. Oates, Stephen B. *Let the Trumpet Sound: The Life of Martin Luther King, Jr.* New York: Harper and Row, 1982. 560 pp., includes bibliography and index, paperback $17.00. ISBN 0-060-92473-X. Oates provides a deeply detailed biography of Martin Luther King, Jr., the slain civil rights leader who received the Nobel Peace Prize in 1964. He traces King's religious, intellectual, and political development and his rise to leadership in the 1960s.

073. Painter, Nell Irvin. *The Narrative of Hosea Hudson, His Life as a Negro Communist in the South.* Cambridge, MA: Harvard University Press, 1979. 400 pp., includes bibliography and index, paperback $17.50. ISBN 0-674-60110-6. This biography divulges the problems Blacks faced in the South during the 1930s and 40s. Painter's exploration of Hudson's life recalls the history of the Communist Party in the South, an almost exclusively Black political movement.

074. Rampersad, Arnold. *The Art and Imagination of W.E.B. DuBois.* New York: Schocken Books, 1990. 323 pp., includes bibliography, $14.95. ISBN 0-805-20985-9. In this "intellectual biography" Rampersad examines DuBois's life and work. He explores DuBois's life as a teacher, essayist, journalist, and civil rights activist as well as an author of autobiography, biography, and fiction. Rampersad highlights DuBois founding of the Niagara Movement, the precursor to the NAACP, as well as his involvement in the early Pan-African movement that culminated in African independence.

075. Rowan, Carl T. *Dream Makers, Dream Breakers: The World of Justice Thurgood Marshall.* Boston, MA: Little, Brown & Co., 1993. 457 pp. Includes bibliography and index, $24.95 hardcover, $12.95 paperback. This is a biography of Thurgood Marshall written by his close friend, Carl Rowan. The book discusses the active part Thurgood Marshall played in his 50-year career. The book talks about his life events including his integral role in the "separate but equal" desegregation movement and his election as the first Black Supreme Court justice in 1967. The book includes many private details, and numerous quotations from interviews and court records.

076. Sadler, Kim M. *Atonement: The Million Man March.* Cleveland, OH: The Pilgrim Press, 1996. 176 pp., paperback $14.95. ISBN 0-82981-147-8. In voices ringing with passion, participants in the Million Man March explore what can be done in their own lives, homes, and communities. The author shares their joys, hopes and pain through

photos, selected speeches, and the voices of participants.   The book includes a resource list of social organizations around the country.

077. Seale, Bobby. *Seize the Time*. New York: Vintage Books, 1991. 429 pp., includes bibliography, $18.95 paperback.   This is a 1960's protest-era classic about the Black Panther Party for Self-Defense. It shows how the Black Panther Party tried to overcome the oppression of Black America through revolutionary methods.   Written by a devoted member of the Black Panthers, this book was mostly completed inside the walls of the San Francisco county jail. The book is not just a history of the Black Panthers but also an objection to the oppression that faces many people around the world.

078. Sterling, Dorothy. *The Making of an Afro-American: Martin Robinson Delany, 1812-1885*. New York: Da Capo Press, 1996. 352 pp., includes bibliography and index, hardcover $14.95. ISBN 0-306-80721-1. The life of Delany, described as the father of Black Nationalism, is chronicled in this biography. Sterling reveals a completely different experience of a Black man in the era of slavery. Through her text, readers can view the life of a Black man who maintained his pride, dignity, and honor in spite of slavery.

079. Terry, Roderick. *One Million Strong: A Photographic Tribute to the Million Man March & Affirmations for the African-American Male*. Edgewater, MD: Duncan and Duncan, 1996. 96 pp., hardcover $24.95. ISBN 1-87864-729-6. Terry explores the Million Man March from a visual perspective. The book includes graphic images of the March through the eyes of the participants.

080. Thompson, Julius E. *Percy Greene and the* Jackson Advocate*: The Life and Times of a Radical Conservative Black Newspaperman, 1897-1977*. Jefferson, NC: McFarland, 1994. Includes bibliography and index. This book is about Percy Greene, editor of *The Advocate* and one of Mississippi's leading journalists of the 20th century. *The Advocate* is the longest running Black newspaper in Mississippi history.   Greene is controversial because he demanded Black voting rights but defended the status quo during the Civil Rights Movement and accepted payoffs for being against civil rights. Greene's story provides a different picture of Blacks during the Civil Rights Movement.

081. Ware, Gilbert. *William Hastie: Grace Under Pressure*. New York: Oxford University Press, 1984. 305 pp., includes bibliography and index, hardcover $39.95. ISBN 0-195-03298-5. Ware provides a thorough

biography of Hastie, a graduate of Amherst College and Harvard Law School who served as a lawyer in the Department of the Interior, governor of the Virgin Islands, and judge in the U.S. Court of Appeals. Ware traces Hastie's membership in the New Negro Alliance and his role in starting the first in a series of lawsuits to ban segregation in public schools for the NAACP.

082. Wilkins, Roy with Mathews, Tom. *Standing Fast: The Autobiography of Roy Wilkins.* New York: Viking Press, 1982. 361 pp., hardcover $16.95. ISBN 0-670-14229-8. Wilkins writes about his nearly 50 years with the NAACP and provides personal and family history. He describes his views of America, integration, and the NAACP programs.

4

Crime, Violence, and Criminal Justice

083. Al Aswadu, A. "A Black View of Prison," *The Black Scholar*, v 2, n 8-9 (1971), pp. 28-31. Aswadu provides an inside look at the bleak circumstances under which Black prisoners live. Very sensitive, yet powerful source.

084. Alan-Williams, Gregory. *A Gathering of Heroes: Reflections on Rage and Responsibility.* Chicago, IL: Academy Chicago Publishers, 1996. 200 pp., $18.95. ISBN 0-89733-404-3. An African-American actor, Alan-Williams deliberately set out for the epicenter of violence during the Los Angeles riots. He was resolute to restrain black anger and save any possible victims of that anger. At the heart of this book is an eyewitness account of the lawlessness and brutality of that day, as well as his rescue of two victims of black anger. Alan-Williams also provides an analysis of his own motives, as well as the brutality of the attackers.

085. Anonymous. "Episodes from the Attica Massacre," *The Black Scholar*, v 4, n 2 (1972), pp. 34-40. This source narrates the crisis that occurred September 9-13, 1971 at Attica Prison in upstate New York. The author tells of how many Blacks were killed in the tragedy and the racial biases held by the troops at the scene, quoted as saying, "I'll kill you niggers."

086. Bedau, Hugh Adam and Pierce, Chester M. (eds.). *Capital Punishment in the United States.* New York: AMS Press, 1976. 567 pp., includes

bibliography and index. ISBN 0-404-10325-1. As a collaboration of essays about capital punishment, this book did a fair job in presenting several different points of view on capital punishment. The source also discusses discretionary judgment that could be used to suppress evidence against Black offenders if it is in their favor.

087. "Black on Black Crime," *Ebony* (August, 1979). This was an entire issue of *Ebony Magazine* dedicated to the reporting and evaluation of Black on Black crime, then a phenomenon of recent appearance. Boasting such articles as "More Blacks Killed on Streets than Vietnam" and "Destruction of the Cities: Crime Plays Big Role in Creating Urban Blight," this was an extremely valuable evaluation of street crimes committed by Blacks against other Blacks.

088. Carter, Dan T. *Scottsboro: A Tragedy of the American South.* Baton Rouge, LA: Louisiana State University Press, 1979. 479 pp., includes bibliography, index, and illustrations. ISBN 0-807-10498-1. This book outlines what happened in 1931 when several White hoboes entered a police station charging that several Black youths had beaten them and pushed one man off of a moving train car. Several Blacks were rounded up without discretion and most were falsely convicted of the crime. All the men were finally pardoned in 1941, but this story is an excellent example of the bias of "justice" against African-Americans.

089. Centers for Disease Control. "Homicide Among Young Black Males-- United States 1970-1982," *Morbidity and Mortality Weekly Report*, v 34, n 41 (1985), pp. 629-633. This study says that Black males aged 15-24 years have the highest rate of homicide, with the highest between the ages of 20-24. It shows that the rates have decreased 33.5% between 1972- 1984 and gives a demographic and situational background of the homicide.

090. Chrisman, R. "Black Prisoners, White Law," *The Black Scholar*, v 2, n 8- 9 (1971), pg. 44-46. This insightful article shows how Whites dominate the prison system and therefore it does not work for Black offenders the way it works for White offenders.

091. Davis, Angela Y. "Rape, Racism, and the Capitalist Setting," *The Black Scholar*, v 9, n 7 (1978), pg. 24-30. Written by the Black feminist scholar, Davis, this article shows how rape laws, originally intended to protect White men whose wives were at risk for rape, are biased in a now deeply entrenched class society based on capitalism. Racist biases have

facilitated the lack of rape convictions against White men and caused more convictions of Black "offenders."

092. Davis, Angela Y. "The Soledad Brothers," *The Black Scholar*, v 2, n 8-9 (1971), pp. 2-7. This article shows how crimes committed by Blacks are penalized differently than those by Whites. This is an excellent source to show the biases of the criminal justice system in America.

093. Donzinger, S. "The Prison Industrial Complex," *Washington Post* (17 March 1996), pp. C-3. This recently article published article describes how, for example, 21 companies in the U.S. manage 88 prisons by contract with the U.S. government. Prisons have basically become a business arrangement propagated by profit-sharing and greed rather than the welfare of the prisons, their families, and the people in those communities.

094. Earls, Felton J. and Reiss, Albert J., Jr. *Breaking the Cycle: Predicting and Preventing Crime*. Washington, DC: United States Department of Justice, Office of Justice Programs, National Institute of Justice, 1994. 66 pp. Shipping list 95-0016-P, monthly catalogue 95063765. This report was conducted by the government to strategically prevent crime. This is a valuable source because it provides both developmental and interdisciplinary perspectives following subjects from birth to adulthood.

095. Fanon, Frantz. *The Wretched of the Earth*. New York: Grove Press, 1986. 255 pp., $12.00. ISBN 0-802-15083-7. Fanon forces his readers to see the Algerian revolution and by analogy to see other contemporary revolutions from the viewpoint of the rebels. Fanon's position is essentially that all crimes committed by both sides in the Algerian war derive from the basic crime of a rule imposed and maintained by violence, and inaccessible to any appeal save that of violence. This book is a Black psychoanalyst's study of the problems of racism and colonialism today.

096. Fingerhut, L.A. and Kleinman, J.C. "International and Interstate Comparison of Homicide Among Young Males," *Journal of the American Medical Association*, v 263, n 24 (1990), pp. 3292-3295. This is a good supplement to the Centers for Disease Control report, "Homicide Among Young Black Males--United States, 1970-1982." It is a very similar report that states very clearly that homicide is the number one killer of young Black men between the ages of 18-25.

097. Humphrey, J.A. and Palmer, S. "Race, Sex and Criminal Homicide-Victim Relationships," in D. Hawkins (ed.), *Homicide Among Black*

Americans, London: University Press of America, 1986, pp. 57-67. ISBN 0-8191-5599-3. This collaboration about crimes by and against Blacks provides excellent hard data as well as perspective on the relationships between victims and their assailants. Includes information on the age, sex, and offender/victim pre-relationship in the subjects studied.

098. Hutchinson, Earl Ofari. *The Mugging of Black America.* Chicago: African-American Images, 1991. 136 pp., paperback $8.95. ISBN 0-913-54321-7. This book focuses on the relationship between race and crime. Hutchinson divides the book into two sections, devoting one to the history of the problems between race and crime, and then developing the second half into a look at the solutions to this problem. He analyzes solutions such as community policing, better use of the media, empowerment of local leaders, greater access to jobs, and the reduced use of prisons. Hutchinson suggests that by using these solutions, crime will be greatly reduced.

099. Jackson, George. *Soledad Brother: The Prison Letters of George Jackson.* Chicago: Lawrence Hill Books, 1994. 339 pp. ISBN 1-556-52230-4. This book tells the story of George Jackson, and more importantly tells the story of Jonathon Jackson, George's brother, and Angela Davis as Soledad Brothers. George Jackson was convicted at the age of 18 of stealing $70, and was sentenced to one year to life in prison. This book tells the rage inside of Jonathon Jackson that drove him to take action in a courthouse. The main issue dealt with in this text is: "How many more Jacksons must pour out their souls in tortured, heavily censored prison letters to convince us of the monstrosity of our system." Jackson reveals the racism in our prisons, and provides evidence of the degradation of Black existence in this society.

100. Jackson, Jesse and Jackson, Jesse, Jr. *Legal Lynching: Racism, Injustice and the Death Penalty.* New York: Marlowe and Company, 1996. 224 pp., includes bibliography and index, hardcover $22.95, paperback $12.95. ISBN 1-569-24761-7 (H), 1-569-24706-4 (P). In a powerful way, the authors make the same arguments that have convinced many nation-states to eliminate capital punishment. Jackson and son discuss the history of the death penalty, and "examine the constitutional, moral, and theological issues that are raised by the death penalty." This text cites cases where innocent people were sentenced to death to further develop the authors' argument that the death penalty presents a risk of innocent people being executed.

101. Mallory, M. "The Framing of Ahmed Evans," *The Black Scholar*, v 2, n 8-9 (1971), pp. 19-23. Showing once again that the U.S. justice system, dominated by White males, has biases that do not seem to allow for valid exposition of important facts as in the case of Ahmed Evans. This article proves thought-provoking criticism of the court system.

102. Miller, Jerome G. *Search and Destroy: African American Males in the Criminal Justice System.* Cambridge, MA: Cambridge University, 1997. 320 pp., includes bibliography and index, hardcover $24.95, paperback $16.95. ISBN 0-521-46021-2 (H), 0-521-59858-3 (P). Using statistics and examples from the criminal justice system, Miller finds that the courts treat crimes committed by Black men with unnecessary severity. He also pinpoints racial bias in public housing, research, and substance abuse prevention.

103. National Advisory Commission on Civil Disorders. *The Kerner Report: The 1968 Report of the National Advisory Commission on Civil Disorders.* New York: Pantheon Books, 1988. 609 pp., includes index. ISBN 0-679-72078-2. A commission of moderate Black leaders, formed by President Johnson in July 1967, The Commission on Civil Disorders created this report. It documents the tough life of the urban poor, where 9.7 million Blacks lived in 1968. The Commission deals with American race riots, what fuels them, and what can be done about them. It recommends specific changes dealing with areas such as jobs, housing, schools, police procedures, and newspaper practices.

104. New York Special Commission on Attica. *Attica: The Official Report of the New York State Special Commission on Attica.* New York: Praeger Publishers, 1972. 533 pp., includes bibliography and index. This report on the Attica massacre explains thoroughly the events behind the insurrection and subsequent massacre.

105. O'Carroll, P.W. and Mercy, J.A. "Patterns and Recent Trends in Black Homicide," in D. Hawkins (ed.), *Homicide Among Black Americans*, London: University of America Press, 1986, pp. 29-42. This source is an easy to read overview of the subject of Black homicide.

106. Oliver, William. *The Violent Social World of Black Men.* New York: Lexington Books, 1994. 195 pp., includes bibliography and index, hardcover $24.95, paperback $22.95. ISBN 0-669-27952-8 (H), 0-787-94305-3 (P). The author conducted a study on violence in the social world of Black men. The study examines the circumstances that lead to arguments and violent confrontations between Black males in social

settings such as bars, clubs, restaurants, and streetcorners. Following the discussion of his findings, Oliver relates his findings to possible methods of preventing interpersonal violence among Black men.

107. Prothrow-Stith,   Deborah   with   Weissman,   Michaele.   *Deadly Consequences*. New York: Harper Collins Publishers, 1991. 269 pp., includes bibliography and index, hardcover $22.50, paperback $13.00. ISBN 0-060-16344-5 (H), 0-060-92402-0 (P). Much recent research in the social sciences finds that urban violence is a problem that cannot simply be turned over to police and prison officials for their attention. In this book, Prothrow-Stith and Weissman contend that teenage violence is a public health problem as well as a problem for the criminal justice system. They reviews the literature on teenage violence and recommends specific plans that require cooperation and innovative problem-solving by a wide range of agencies.

108. Reiss, Albert J. and Roth, J.A. (eds.). *Understanding and Preventing Violence*. Washington, D.C.: National Academy Press, 1993. 464 pp., hardcover $49.95, paperback $24.95. ISBN 0-336-04594-0 (H), 0-309-05476-1 (P). The National Research Council formed a panel to study violent behavior. This collection is a summary of the documents they used in their research. The book examines and discusses many of the trends of violent behavior. While examining and discrediting myths, the book gives evidences such as circumstances, environment, biology, and psychology as reasons for violent behavior. The panel, based on these explanations, made four recommendations for preventing violence. These include increased intervention, expanded information systems, new research topics, and community development studies.

109. Shakur, Sanyika. *Monster: The Autobiography of an L.A. Gang Member*. New York: Penguin Books, 1993. 382 pp., paperback $12.95. ISBN 0-14023-225-7. Shakur provides a shockingly raw, frightening portrait of gang life in South Central Los Angeles. This autobiography chronicles his life as a brutal gang member through his personal transformation in prison to a Black nationalist and crusader against the causes of gangsterism.

110. Sienko, D.G., Thursh, J. and Wilcox, K.R. "Impact of Homicide on Years of Potential Life Lost in Michigan's Black Population," *Journal of the American Medical Association*, v 261, n 5 (1989), pp. 686-687. JAMA provided extensive and laymen friendly research on homicide, describing how Black men have more average "years of potential life lost" due to

homicide rates among urban Blacks. This article emphasizes that young Blacks are dying fast.

111. Spain, J. "The Black Family and the Prisons," *The Black Scholar*, v 4, n 2 (1972), pp. 18-31. The author, then a member of the Black Panther Party, was one of the infamous San Quentin Six who was charged with the killing of three guards and two inmates in a supposed escape attempt. Spain asserts that being poor, Black or both makes one unimportant to the "Ameriklan" society and therefore unworthy of rehabilitation and respect while in prison.

112. Tardiff, K., Gross, E.M., and Messner, S.F. "A Study of Homicides in Manhattan," *American Journal of Public Health*, v 76, n 2 (1981), pp. 139-143. This is a very technical article, but interesting no less. The authors study young Black men's life span as compared with other racial groups.

113. Upchurch, Carl. *Convicted in the Womb: One Man's Journey from Prisoner to Peacemaker*. New York: Bantam Books, 1996. 236 pp., hardcover $21.95, paperback $12.95. ISBN 0-553-09726-1 (H), 0-553-37520-2 (P). A product of a Philadelphia ghetto, Upchurch tells the story of his "niggerization" as a teen criminal, and his time in prison and "deniggerization." He also recounts how he changed his life following ten years in prison and his current work of "antiniggerization," and challenging African-Americans to take a stand and shape today's society.

114. Wade, W. "The Politics of Prisons," *The Black Scholar*, v 2, n 8-9 (1971), pp. 12-18. Wade says that politics play an important role in decisions in prisons. Rather than merit, experience or other important factors, personal politics such as racism and sexism play a major role in decisions.

5

Economic Development

115. Anderson, Jervis. *A. Philip Randolph: A Biographical Portrait*. New York: Harcourt Brace Jovanovich, 1973. 398 pp., includes index, $12.50. ISBN 0-15-107830-0. Anderson provides the first full-length study of Randolph, one of the most significant figures in the history of American Socialism, the history of the American labor movement, and the history of Black Americans. Anderson traces his long struggle to organize Black Pullman porters and continues through his involvement in the struggle for Black civil rights through the 1950s.

116. Carrol, John M. *Fritz Pollard: Pioneer in Racial Advancement*. Chicago: University of Illinois Press, 1991. 298 pp., includes bibliography and index. ISBN 0-252-01814-1. This book chronicles the life of Fritz Pollard. It primarily focuses on his accomplishments in athletics and his contributions and commitment to the Civil Rights Movement. It also chronicles his accomplishments in business along with his many "firsts" as an African-American.

117. Case, Frederick E. *Black Capitalism: Problems in Development; A Case Study of Los Angeles*. New York: Praeger Publishers, 1972. 86 pp., includes bibliography. Case focuses on the economic revival of urban minority communities after the 1965 riots in South Central Los Angeles. His book details the Haynes Foundation grant that was used to analyze efforts to revive economic potential in the Black community. The

analysis concentrated on two goals: one to improve employment opportunities, the other to foster more Black-owned and operated businesses.

118. Chavers-Wright, Madrue. *The Guarantee: P.W. Chavers: Banker, Entrepreneur, Philanthropist in Chicago's Black Belt of the Twenties.* New York: Wright-Armstead Associates, 1985. 425 pp., includes bibliography and index. ISBN 0-931-50505-4 (H), 0-931-50504-6 (P). This book discusses the life and achievements of P.W. Chavers in business and philanthropy in 1920s Chicago. His contributions in politics and his "firsts" in banking and other business ventures are chronicled as is the effect of the Depression and where the family and the wealth is today. This is an intimate view of Chavers given by a family member.

119. Denby, Charles. *Indignant Heart: A Black Worker's Journal.* Detroit: Wayne State University Press, 1989. 303 pp., hardcover $35.00, paperback $17.95. ISBN 0-814-32219-0 (H), 0-814-32220-4 (P). This book is divided into two sections and the current edition is an expansion of Denby's original 1952 text. The differences between the two parts are significant, indicating the levels of maturity, sophistication, and personal development Denby went through in the years between 1952-1978. In looking at the changes that occurred in history during this period, the differences in the sections are understandable. This eyewitness account details the changes that occurred as a result of the Civil Rights Movement of the 1960s. In explaining the changes, Denby painfully reminds the reader of the events that occurred during this period.

120. Foner, Philip S. *Organized Labor and the Black Worker, 1619-1981.* New York: International Publishers, 1981. 489 pp. ISBN 0-717-80601-4. This book details the exclusionary history of organized labor with respect to Black populations. It traces the harsh effects of racism on organized labor. Foner argues that Black workers continued to struggle to achieve equality as members of the labor force after the barriers of segregation were removed.

121. Green, Shelly S. and Pride, Paul. *Black Entrepreneurship in America.* New Brunswick, NJ: Transaction Publishers, 1996. 203 pp., includes bibliography, paperback $21.95. IBSN 1-560-00885-7. This book is a calling to the African-American community to look to entrepreneurship to improve the economic condition of the community. The authors argue that Blacks lack entrepreneurship, a key ingredient of economic progress, and thus are more likely to remain impoverished as a community.

122. Greenberg, Jonathan D. *Staking a Claim: Jake Simmons and the Making of an African-American Oil Dynasty.* New York: Atheneum, 1990. 311 pp., includes bibliography and index. ISBN 0-689-11791-4. This is a biography of Jake Simmons that traces his rise to prominence in the oil business, as an oil broker, and his contributions to the Civil Rights Movement. The book also discusses his political prominence. The book gives a good account of how perseverance, determination, honesty, and hard work are important parts of success.

123. Herbert, James I. *Black Male Entrepreneurs and Adult Development.* Westport, CT: Greenwood Press, 1989. 253 pp., includes bibliography and index, hardcover $59.95. ISBN 0-275-93023-8. Herbert's study involves an intensive investigation of ten Black male entrepreneurs who have lived through very significant changes in race relations in the United States. His text is directly relevant to theories of adult development.

124. Hill, George H. *Black Business and Economics: A Selected Annotated Bibliography.* New York: Garland Publishing Co., 1985. 351 pp., includes index. ISBN 0-824-08787-9. This book describes African-American business enterprises and how they evolved. It also contains facts on important African-American businessmen and employment.

125. Hudson, Hosea. *Black Worker in the Deep South: A Personal Record.* New York: International Publishing Co., 1991. 130 pp., hardcover $6.95. ISBN 0-717-80683-9. Hudson's autobiography details his life as a steelworker in Alabama from the 1930s to 1950s. He explains the exploitation and discrimination that drove him to the union movement and the Communist Party.

126. Hund, James M. *Black Entrepreneurship.* Belmont, CA: Wadsworth, 1970. 157 pp., includes bibliography. This book is a collection of profiles of African-American business people. It provides biographical information as it details the events that led to their successes.

127. Ingham, John N. and Feldman, Lynne B. *African-American Business Leaders: A Biographical Dictionary.* Westport, CT: Greenwood Press, 1993. 824 pp., includes index and bibliography, $115.00. ISBN 0-313-27253-0. This book provides biographical profiles of 123 African-Americans in the arena of business. The selected biographies cover achievements by African-Americans in the fields of financial services, retail and service industries, publishing, advertising, broadcasting, manufacturing, real estate, construction, and agriculture.

128. Jaynes, Gerald David. *Branches without Roots: Genesis of the Black Working Class in the American South, 1862-1882.* New York, NY: Oxford University Press, 1989. 351 pp., includes index, paperback $20.00. ISBN 0-195-05575-6. Jaynes looks at the transition from slavery to freedom. He explores the emergence and development of the Black working class and addresses its relation to White society.

129. Lewis, Reginald F. and Walker, Blair S. *"Why Should White Guys Have all the Fun?": How Reginald Lewis Created a Billion-Dollar Business Empire.* New York: John Wiley & Sons, Inc., 1995. 318 pp., includes bibliography, paperback $22.95. ISBN 0-471-04227-7. This book is a biography of Reginald Lewis. It chronicles his life from childhood in Baltimore to prominence in New York. It highlights his business achievements, notably his purchase of Beatrice International Foods. It also chronicles the obstacles, racial and otherwise, that he overcame throughout his life until his death in 1993.

130. Plater, Michael A. *African-American Entrepreneurship in Richmond, 1890-1940: The Story of R.C. Scott.* New York: Garland Publishing, Inc., 1996. 191 pages, includes bibliography and index. ISBN 0-815-32673-4. This book looks at African-American entrepreneurship in the early part of this century in Richmond, Virginia. It discusses its rise and fall by focusing on two industries, funeral homes and cemeteries, and R.C. Scott, their owner. It looks at the impact of history and segregation on the options open to Black businesses, and how the changes in time have affected historically Black businesses.

131. Seder, John and Burrell, B.G. *Getting it Together: Black Businessmen in America.* New York: Harcourt Brace Jovanovich, 1971. 256 pp., includes bibliography. ISBN 0-151-35275-5. This book talks about the business practices of Black America. The book starts with a short history of Black business in Africa and the U.S. from colonial times to the present. Most of the book involves stories from 16 businessmen who succeeded in different areas. The book also points out that Blacks constitute 12% of the population, but only own 1% of the businesses. The book lists different ways to handle the economic problems and gives possible solutions to the Black economic dilemma.

132. Weems, Robert E., Jr. *Black Business in the Black Metropolitan: The Chicago Metropolitan Assurance Company.* Bloomington: Indiana University Press, 1996. 158 pp., $35.00. ISBN 0-253-33025-4. Weems researches America's oldest Black-owned business, The Chicago

Metropolitan Assurance Company, and the various programs and projects established by the company to enhance Black community life.

133. Wier, Sadye H. with Marszalek, John F. *A Black Businessman in White Mississippi, 1886-1974.* Jackson: University of Mississippi, 1977. 79 pp., includes bibliography and index. ISBN 0-878-05042-6. This is a wife's memoir of a Black man in a small Mississippi town during a major part of the twentieth century. Wier tells the life of an unknown Black businessman and leader, her husband, in Mississippi through the days of segregation into the period of integration.

6

Education

134. Gordon, Jacob U. "Key Public Policy Issues in African-American Education," *Journal of Law and Public Policy*, 1992, pp. 49-60. The essay traces major public policy issues in African-American education including the separate but equal doctrine in the case of *Plessy v. Ferguson* in 1896 and the 1954 Supreme Court case of *Brown v. Topeka Board of Education*.

135. Hale-Benson, Janice E. *Black Children: Their Roots, Culture, and Learning Styles*. Baltimore, MD: Johns Hopkins University Press, 1988. 215 pp., includes bibliography and index, paperback $14.95. ISBN 0-842-52092-9. Hale is an associate professor at Jackson State University in Mississippi. She talks about the skills Black children need to acquire in the classroom in order to function in society. She also discussed how Blacks are being "miseducated" in the school system. Hale also offers ideas for different settings that can improve the Black child's behavior and strengthen Black families.

136. Hopkins, Ronnie. *Educating Black Males: Critical Lessons in Schooling, Community, and Power*. A volume in the SUNY series, *Urban Voices, Urban Visions*, Diane DuBose Brunner and Rashidah Jaami' Muhammad, editors. Albany: State University of New York Press, 1997. 192 pp., hardcover $49.50, paperback $16.95. ISBN 0-7914-3157-6 (H), 0-7914-3158-4 (P). Hopkins discusses strategies for creating more effective and

empowering schools and classrooms for Black males. Hopkins examines the social status of African-American males as well as analyzes theoretical contexts of educational theory and practice in crisis intervention and alternative education programs for Black males. The author suggests strategies for motivating learning and improving self-esteem in Black males.

137.   Kozol, Jonathan. *Death at an Early Age: The Destruction of the Hearts and Minds of Negro Children in the Boston Public Schools.* Boston: Houghton-Mifflin Co., 1990. 227 pp., paperback $12.95. ISBN 0-452-26292-5. Kozol describes the scenes of abuse, neglect and discrimination that African-American children were subjected to in 1960's Boston school system. White administrators were obsessed with disciple and cruelty, and were quite willing to ignore massive inequality in education. Kozol explores how inferior education subjects the Black student to an internalized feeling of inferiority, and what impact this has on the Black population.

138.   Ladson-Billings, Gloria. *The Dreamkeepers: Successful Teachers of African-American Children.*   San Francisco: Jossey-Bass Publishers, 1994. 192 pp., paperback $17.00. ISBN 1-555-42668-9 (H), 0-787-90338-8 (P). Gloria Ladson-Billings' account of what it takes to be a successful teacher of black children attempts to focus on the methods of strengthening the identity of African-American schoolchildren. Ladson-Billings centers on eight teachers and the strategies they use to rescue African-American children from historical discrimination. These teachers give a how-to account of accomplishing the goals of educating African-American children.

139.   Morris, Gabrielle. *Head of the Class: An Oral History of African-American Achievement in Higher Education and Beyond.* New York: Simon and Schuster, 1995. 164 pp. ISBN 0-805-79129-9 (H), 0-805-79130-2 (P). This book is a part of the Twayne's Oral History series. Morris interviews the first Black graduates of the University of California at Berkeley and explores their struggles and successes from their perspective. Educational and inspiring, this book explains how these individuals overcame racial barriers to earn their education.

140.   Taylor, George R. *Curriculum Strategies: Social Skills Intervention for Young African-American Males.* Westport, CT: Praeger, 1997. 175 pp., includes bibliography and index, hardcover $49.95. ISBN 0-275-95200-2. This book was created as a guide to help educators instruct young Black males on how to determine moral behavior. This book is designed

for educators and family members to use in their daily interactions and activities with young Black males.

141. Watson, Clifford and Smitherman, Geneva. *Educating African American Males: Detroit's Malcolm X Academy Solution.* Chicago: Third World Press. 128 pp., hardcover $29.95, paperback $12.95. ISBN 0-883-78185-9 (H), 0-883-78157-3 (P). The Malcolm X Academy attempts to solve, through African centered curriculum, low educational standards and outcomes of African-American males. This book explains the school's philosophy and curriculum as it explains the success of their program.

142. Wilson, Chuckie. *Study of the African-American Male in the Academic Setting in Kansas City, Kansas Public Schools.* Topeka, KS: Kansas State Board of Education, 1991. 64 pp. Wilson examines the socioeconomic factors impacting the education of African-American males in Kansas City, Kansas. Wilson analyzes the connection between low educational performance and crime, juvenile delinquency, and unemployment.

7

Family

143. Alston, Harvey. *Black Males: An African-American View on Raising Young Men.* Dubuque, IA: Kendall/Hunt Publishing Co., 1994. 148 pp., paperback $16.95. ISBN 0-840-38482-9. Harvey examines the impact of slavery on the African-American family. Alston offers suggestions to parents for motivating their sons and instilling a sense of national identity. This book is about pride, heritage, and integrity.

144. Austin, Bobby (ed.). *Repairing the Breach: Key Ways to Support Family Life, Reclaim our Streets, and Rebuild Civil Society in America's Communities.* Chicago: Noble Press, 1996. 204 pp., includes bibliography and index, paperback $14.95. ISBN 1-879-36045-4. This report of the National Task Force on African-American Men and Boys raises critical issues about the plight of African-American males in American society. The book also recommends processes for empowering the African-American male.

145. Bernard, J. *Marriage and Family among Negroes.* Englewood Cliffs, NJ: Prentice-Hall, 1966. 160 pp. An American sociologist, Bernard dissects Black family life as he examines how Black families deviate from White family norms. Black urbanization and self-emancipation are ongoing themes in this book. Bernard also points out the huge gap in knowledge about contemporary Black marriage and family life.

146. Billingsley, Andrew. *Black Families in White America*. Englewood Cliffs, NJ: Prentice-Hall Publishers, 1988. 218 pp., includes bibliography and index. ISBN 0-671-67162-6. In this book, Billingsley updates E. Franklin Frazier's classic study, *The Negro Family in the United States*. Billingsley contends that the improvement of Black family life depends on the decrease of racism and the rejection of the Moynihan report.

147. Blankenhorn, David. *Fatherless America: Confronting Our Most Urgent Social Problem*. New York: Basic Books/Harper Collins, 1995. 352 pp., includes index, hardcover $23.00. ISBN 0-465-01483-6. Blankenhorn identifies an increase in the number of families without fathers, and theorizes this has led to higher incidences of crime, domestic violence, child sexual abuse, and child poverty. He also discusses the impact of this cultural phenomenon. Blankenhorn examines eight significant father roles in American society. He also offers 12 strategies to redefine the role of fatherhood.

148. Braden, Warren. *Homies: Peer Mentoring Among African-American Males*. Dekalb, IL: LEPS Press of Northern Illinois University, 1998. 200 pp., paperback $15.95. ISBN 1-879528-14-2. *Homies* is a study of a group of African-American men from the Chicago West Side. This book tries to explain the bond of communication between these men. It exposes the social contribution of their alternative reality and explores its rationality. The book describes two differing homie cultures: "book smart" and "street smart." Braden explores various themes related to the homie subculture.

149. Cosby, Bill. *Fatherhood*. Berkley Publishing Group, 1994. 178 pp., paperback $11.95. ISBN 0-425-09772-2. Cosby's "advice on surviving the vagaries of one's offspring consists of a succession of...anecdotes and observations, all designed to encourage the application of love and patience." Cosby's *Fatherhood* is charming and amusing. If you like his comedy, you'll like his book.

150. Frazier, E. Franklin. *The Negro Family in the United States*. Chicago: University of Chicago Press, 1940. 686 pp., includes bibliography. ISBN 0-226-26141-7. In this classic study, Franklin writes a history of the Black family from slavery to the present. The book contains case histories and statistical tables. He illuminates the process of social change and the treatment of the Black family in the United States. Dr. Frazier reveals wide variations of social classes among the Black population. He also sheds light on Black education, business, industry, and housing.

151. Gary, Lawrence E., Beatty, L.A., Berry, G.L., and Price, M.D. *Stable Black Families: Final Report.* Washington, DC: Institute for Urban Affairs and Research, 1983. 92 pp., includes bibliography. Gary conducted a study of fifty families in the Washington, DC area--26 husband-wife and 24 female headed families. In total, seventy-six individuals were interviewed to determine the critical factors and conditions that contribute to strong Black family life. Gary found that the problems most frequently reported were finances, marriage, and children.

152. Gilbert, Roland and Tyehimba-Taylor, Cheo. *The Ghetto Solution: African-American Boys Learning How to Become African-American Men.* Waco, Texas: WRS Publishing, 1993. 208 pp., $19.95. ISBN 1-56796-021-9. A reformed convict and crack addict, Gilbert offers a combination of religious and self-help skills to guide children in the urban core. He is the creator of a seminar program called SIMBA (Safe In My Brother's Arms) for young Black men. He uses the Afrocentric rites-of-passage to enable young men to resolve conflict and successfully transition to adulthood.

153. Golden, Marita. *Saving Our Sons: Raising Black Children in a Turbulent World.* New York: Doubleday, 1995. 208 pp., hardcover $18.50, paperback $10.95. ISBN 0-385-47302-8 (H), 0-385-47303-6 (P). In this autobiographical testimony, novelist Golden combines diary entries with her thoughts on what it means to parent an adolescent Black male in the turbulence of today's society. In her writing, she makes the problems of racism, crime and violence, and parenting very real.

154. Gutman, Herbert G. *The Black Family in Slavery and Freedom.* New York: Random House, 1977. 664 pp., includes index, paperback $24.00 ISBN 0-394-72451-8. Gutman conducted a study of the Afro-American family between 1750-1925 as well as the origins and early development of their culture. This study was stimulated by the controversy surrounding Daniel P. Moynihan's *The Negro Family in America.* This study is an examination of the Afro-American family prior to and after the general emancipation. In addition, it also studies the cultural beliefs and behavior of a distinctive lower-class population.

155. Hare, Nathan and Hare, Julia. *Bringing the Black Boy to Manhood: The Passage.* San Francisco: The Black Think Tank, 1985. 38 pp., paperback $5.00. ISBN 0-961-30861-3. The authors have created a self-help manual for young Black males. This book will have a positive influence on all children.

156. Hill, Odeather Allen. *African-American Young Men Transition Towards Independent Living: A Case Study*. New York: Vantage Press, 1998. Paperback $10.95. ISBN 0-533-12291-0. The author deals with the issue of African-American males being an endangered species. Hill examines the impact of socioeconomic factors on the Black family and provides steps for improving the lives of young Black men.

157. Hutchinson, Earl Ofari. *Black Fatherhood: The Guide to Male Parenting*. Los Angeles, CA: Middle Passage Press, 1992. 143 pp., includes bibliography and index, paperback $11.95. ISBN 1-881-03209-4. Hutchinson's book is a guide that offers advice on supporting the healthy development of African-American boys. The topics discussed include education, health and communication. The author illustrates his study with examples from African-American fathers.

158. Hutchinson, Earl Ofari. *Black Fatherhood II: Black Women Talk about their Men*. Los Angeles, CA: Middle Passage Press, 1994. 173 pp., paperback $11.95. ISBN 1-881-03210-8. A follow-up to *Black Fatherhood*, this book addresses the challenges of interpersonal relationships. The women talk about their fathers and other significant male figures. The book reveals negative opinions some Black women have of Black men.

159. Jones, Lealan and Newman, Lloyd with Isay, David. *Our America: Life and Death on the South Side of Chicago*. New York: Scribner, 1997. 203 pp., hardcover $23.00, paperback $14.00. ISBN 0-684-83616-5 (H), 0-671-00464-6 (P). This text describes life in Chicago's Ida B. Wells Home. Jones and Newman demonstrate the gulf between mainstream life and life in the urban core.

160. Kunjufu, Jawanza. *Countering the Conspiracy to Destroy Black Boys: Volumes 1, 2 and 3*. Chicago: African American Images, 1985, 1986, 1990. Paperback $6.95 (each). IBSN 0-913-54300-4 (v1), 0-913-54303-9 (v2), 0-913-54320-9 (v3). This text is available in three separate short volumes. The books examine the conspiracy to keep African-American men from succeeding. Kunjufu examines the government treaties and cultural habits that contribute to the conspiracy. He looks at relationships between mothers and sons, Black male educational experiences, and rites of passage programs.

161. Kunjufu, Jawanza. *Developing Positive Self-Images and Discipline in Black Children*. Chicago: African American Images, 1984. 105 pp., includes bibliography and index, paperback $8.95. ISBN 0-913-54301-2.

Kunjufu explores strategies for Black male education that are rooted in educational theory. He offers viable approaches for teachers, parents, and families.

162. Majors, Richard and Wiener, Susan. *Programs that Serve African-American Male Youth.* Washington, D.C.: Urban Institute Press, 1995. 100 pp., $13.50. This publication offers a description of programs for young Black males and adolescents in urban society. 60 programs in 40 states are highlighted. The authors provide contact information for various programs.

163. Marshall, Joseph, Jr. and Wheeler, Lonnie. *Street Soldier: One Man's Struggle To Save a Generation--One Life at a Time.* New York: Delacorte Press, 1996. 336 pp., $22.95. ISBN 0-385-31430-2. Marshall heads San Francisco's Omega Boys Club, which he founded in 1987 with Jack Jacqna to help at-risk youth. Marshall works to eliminate violent crime, drug abuse, and unemployment as he advocates education, employment, and self-respect through his Club. In this book, he offers key principles to live by and rules for survival.

164. McAdoo, Harriett Pipes (ed.). *Black Families.* Beverly Hills, CA: Sage Publications, 1996. 323 pp., includes bibliography and index, hardcover $59.95, paperback $25.95. ISBN 0-803-95572-3 (H), 0-803-95573-1 (P). This book consists of twenty-one categorized essays that focus on aspects of the Black family ranging from parenting to family values and public policy.

165. McBride, James. *The Color of Water: A Black Man's Tribute to His White Mother.* New York: Riverhead Books, 1996. 228 pp., includes bibliography, hardcover $22.95, paperback $12.00. ISBN 1-573-22022-1 (H), 1-573-22578-9 (P). The author tells the story of his White mother and his own search for identity as a biracial American. This book illustrates the parallels between two seemingly different cultures and ultimately demonstrates that race and religion are transcended by family love.

166. Mincy, Ronald B. (ed.). *Nurturing Young Black Males: Challenges to Agencies, Programs, and Social Policy.* Washington, D.C.: Urban Institute Press, 1994. 260 pp., hardcover $19.95. ISBN 0-87766-598-2. A collection of essays focusing on the conditions facing many adolescent Black males--involvement in crime and violence, vulnerability to dropping out of school, and susceptibility to drug and alcohol abuse.

Mincy focuses on intervention programs, policy changes, and risk factors that impact young Black men.

167. Perkins, Useni Eugene. *Harvesting New Generations: The Positive Development of Black Youths.* Chicago: Third World Press, 1993. 240 pp., paperback $12.95. ISBN 0-883-78116-6. Perkins' sequel to 'Home is a Dirty Place' provides a positive outlook on how Black youth can flourish beyond what Perkins calls "ghettocolony." He argues that oppression establishes unity and values. Perkins provides ideas for improving the lives of future generations.

168. Rainwater, Lee. *Behind Ghetto Walls: Black Life in a Federal Slum.* Chicago: Aldine Publishing Company, 1972. 446 pp., includes bibliography, hardcover $12.50. ISBN 0-202-30113-3. Based on a six-year study of the private lives of 10,000 Black people in a federal housing project in St. Louis, this book includes extensive interviews with individual families.

169. Sanders, Herman A. *Daddy, We Need you Now!: A Primer on African-American Male Socialization.* Lanham, MD: University Press of America, 1996. ISBN 0-761-80379-3 (H) 0-761-80380-7 (P). Sanders encapsulates the growing problem that many Black families face: the loss of their male figures. Other subjects covered include the social conditions and psychology of the Black male. Sanders explores the impact of drugs, imprisonment, and gangs on Black families.

170. Stack, Carol B. *All Our Kin: Strategies for Survival in a Black Community.* New York: Basic Books, 1997. 192 pp., includes bibliography. ISBN 0-061-31982-1. This book focuses on how African-Americans survive in a community that is "severely deprived." Stack compares Black and White families and finds that kinship values and the sharing of resources are the primary reasons for the survival of African-American communities.

171. Staples, Robert. *The Black Family: Essays and Studies.* Belmont, CA: Wadsworth Publishing Co., 1998. 249 pp., paperback $34.95. ISBN 0-534-55296-X. Staples captures the essence of the Black family in this book. Covering such subjects as social conditions and Black sociology he discusses what the Black family is all about. With case studies as the groundwork, Staples grasps the idea of family, work, and relationships and what role they play in the Black family.

172. U.S. Department of Labor. *The Negro Family: The Case for National Action*. Westport, CT: Greenwood Press, 1981. ISBN 0-313-22853-1. Commonly known as "The Moynihan Report," this text discusses Black family structure. Moynihan discusses social conditions as well as the problems that confront Black families. He looks at the nation's efforts to establish a stable structure for the Black family.

173. Wideman, John Edgar. *Fatheralong: A Meditation on Fathers and Sons, Race and Society*. New York: Pantheon Books, 1994. 197 pp., hardcover $21.00, paperback $13.00. ISBN 0-679-40720-0 (H), 0-679-73751-0 (P). In five inter-related essays, Wideman explores connection and division, commonality and difference, emotions experienced directly and understandings haltingly achieved. He discusses the long, troubled history of his interactions with his father, father-son links in general, and other kinds of relationships. Wideman asserts that race has little to do with color or culture and everything to do with power.

174. Willis, Andre C. (ed.). *Faith of Our Fathers: African-American Men Reflect on Fatherhood*. New York: Penguin Books USA, Inc., 1996. 227 pp., hardcover $22.95, paperback $11.95. ISBN 0-525-94158-4 (H), 0-452-27669-1 (P). A collection of 12 original essays that offer a survey of the range and challenges of black fatherhood, told from the perspectives of fathers and sons. Contributors include well known scholars and Black men such as Cornel West, Robin D.G. Kelley, John Edgar Wideman, Anthony Cook, Delfeayo Marsalis, Michael G. Hanchard, and Playthall Benjamin. Contributions include personal stories as well as an evaluation of the impact of media stereotypes, family values, and economic development on the Black family.

8

Gender and Masculinity

175. Belton, Don (ed.). *Speak My Name: Black Men on Masculinity and the American Dream.* Boston, Massachusetts: Beacon Press, 1995. 264 pp., $24.00. ISBN 0-8070-0936-9. An anthology touching upon African-American men's family life, self-image, and personal relationships. These writings focus on the image of the Black man from the point of view of the Black man himself. Thirty well-known poets, writers, and storytellers write about the Million Man March and give autobiographical accounts of men growing up Black in America. The essays explore topics such as racism, injustice, family, love, marriage, and survival.

176. Clatterbaugh, Kenneth C. *Contemporary Perspectives on Masculinity: Men, Women, and Politics in Modern Society.* Boulder, CO: Westview Press, 1997. 242 pages, includes bibliography and index, hardcover $69.95, paperback $19.95. ISBN 0-813-32700-8 (H), 0-813-32701-6 (P). Clatterbaugh addresses what masculinity means in modern times. He uses six theoretical approaches--conservative, pro-feminist, group-specific, men's rights, spiritual, and socialist--to discuss issues and problems men face. Clatterbaugh's goal is to outline a way to improve men's "reality" within the context of U.S. culture.

177. Connor, Marlene K. *What is Cool?: Understanding Black Manhood in America.* New York: Crown Publishers, 1995. 224 pp., $20.00. ISBN 0-517-79965-0. Connor asserts that cool is "perhaps the most important

force in the life of a man in black America." She proceeds through four forms of "cool": "Street Cool," the survival mechanism for inner city life; "Revolutionary Cool," that associated with the racial pride born in the 1960s; "Middle-class Cool," the survival mechanism in White workplaces and White campuses; and "Electronic Cool," as found in the media. She notes that cool has hampered relations between Black women and men, and warns that in a diverse society the idea of cool can be a limiting self-definition.

178. Harper, Phillip Brian. *Are We Not Men?: Masculine Anxiety and the Problem of African-American Identity*. New York: Oxford University Press, 1996. 254 pp., includes bibliography and index, $25.00. ISBN 0-19-509274-0. A collection of eight essays in which Harper investigates traditional definitions of race, gender and class and how they impact African-American male life and identity. He analyzes ways in which Black masculine identity affects American culture.

179. Hernton, Calvin C. *Sex and Racism in America*. New York: Anchor, 1992. 208 pp., includes bibliography, paperback $12.00. ISBN 0-385-42433-7. A sociologist, Hernton identifies sexual paranoia and persecution as major factors in racial prejudice. In separate chapters on the White woman, the Black man, the White Man, and the Black woman, he discusses how each views themselves and the others.

180. Kimmel, Michael S. and Messner, Michael A. *Men's Lives*. Needham Heights, MA: Allyn and Bacon, 1998. 536 pp. ISBN 0-205-26649-5 (P). A collection of 57 articles considering male gender role issues. Within the major sections, articles explore issues from several vantage points, including that of African-American males. This third edition has new articles from the African-American perspective.

181. Madhubuti, Haki R. *Black Men: Obsolete, Single, Dangerous? The Afrikan American Family in Transition: Essay in Discovery, Solution and Hope*. Chicago: Third World Press, 1990. 273 pp., includes bibliography, hardcover $14.95. ISBN 0-883-78135-2. Madhubuti, a Black writer and poet, sheds light on the Black man's problems. Through essays and poems he confronts the myth and hypocrisy of the Black man's societal position, and urges change.

182. Majors, Richard and Billson, Janet Mancini. *Cool Pose: The Dilemmas of Black Manhood in America*. New York: Lexington Books, 1992. 144 pp., hardcover $21.95, paperback $12.00. ISBN 0-669-24523-2 (H), 0-671-86572-2 (P). The authors explore the condition of young Black

males and Black men by examining a common psychological stance, "cool pose," taken toward living under oppressive conditions. They address two questions: how this stance helps bring balance, stability, confidence, and a sense of masculinity to African-American males; and how this stance works destructively in their lives. They offer suggestions for future research and policy change through a broadening of perspectives on the dilemmas of Black manhood.

183. Staples, Robert. *Black Masculinity: The Black Male's Role in American Society*. San Francisco: The Black Scholar Press, 1982. 272 pp., includes bibliography and index, paperback $11.95. IBSN 0-933-29606-1. This is the second book in a trilogy. It examines Black males' conflicting relationship with society's definition of maleness. Mostly rewritten articles, the text concentrates on contemporary urban subjects. It combines many different views in exploring the subject, including neo-Marxism and Pan Africanism. The book also claims that Black men are casualties of the women's movement.

184. Wallace, Michele. *Black Macho and the Myth of the Superwoman*. New York: Dial Press, 1990. 228 pp., includes bibliography and index, paperback $18.00. ISBN 0-860-91518-2. Wallace focuses on the changes in the Black community since 1968 as reported by a series of articles published in *The New York Times*. The articles covered the Civil Rights Movement and the economic conditions of the Black community. Her book is best known for her argument that "Black Macho" and interracial relationships helped destroy the Black Power Movement.

9

Health and Mental Health

185. Dennis, Ruth. "Social Stress and Mortality Among Non-White Males," *Phylon*, v 38, pp. 315-327. Ms. Dennis lists and portrays the leading mortality trends among young Black males, discusses some of the emerging sociocultural factors linked to increased mortality rates and suggests means of lowering the mortality rate. She suggests that methods to decreasing social stress or improving coping might be found in the Black church, school, business, and social organizations.

186. Evans, Brenda J. and Whitfield, James. R. *Black Males in the United States: An Annotated Bibliography from 1967 to 1987.* Washington, DC: American Psychological Association, 1988. 152 pp., paperback $25.00. ISBN 1-557-98404-3. An annotated bibliography of psychological journal literature and dissertations found in PsycINFO that focus on Black Males in the United States. Articles and dissertations are divided by area of psychology (e.g. psychometric, experimental, physiological, developmental, social processes & social issues, personality, educational, applied, and etc.).

187. Fullilove, Robert E., Fullilove, Mindy T., Bowser, Benjamin P., and Gross, Shirley A. "Risk of Sexually Transmitted Diseases Among Black, Adolescent Crack Users in Oakland and San Francisco, California," *Journal of the American Medical Association*, v 263, February 1990, pp. 851-855. In an exploratory cross-sectional study, the authors examine the

connection between crack cocaine use and the incidence of sexually transmitted disease among Black teenagers.

188. Geerken, M. and Gove, W. "Race, Sex, and Marital Status: The Effect on Mortality," *Social Problems*, v 21 (4), 1974, pp. 567-580. The hypothesis exists that Black families tend to have a matrifocal structure. In an effort to test this idea, the authors compared mortality rates for Blacks and Whites across sex and marital status, including types of mortality due to psychosocial stress. Results showed no great differences in marital roles' relation to mortality rate. However, the small difference that did exist suggested that marriage is better for White men and Black women. The data also suggested that unmarried status is best for the Black man.

189. Heckler, Margaret. *Report of the Secretary's Task Force on Black and Minority Health*. Bethesda, MD: U.S. Department of Health and Human Services, 1985. 549 pp. Margaret Heckler, Secretary of Health and Human Services, compiled this report on the American public's health that focuses on minority groups. The document concentrates on the disparity between the health of White Americans and that of minority groups. The report aims to set a framework for improving the minority group health.

190. Jackson, James S. (ed.). *The Black American Elderly: Research on Physical and Psychosocial Health*. New York: Springer, 1988. 383 pp., includes bibliography, hardcover $43.95. ISBN 0-826-15810-2. In 1984 and 1985 the National Institute on Aging presented a workshop entitled "Research on Aging Black Populations." This five-part collection is based on that series of workshops. Twenty authors discuss issues pertinent to aging Blacks. Topics include increased funding and involvement in the research on Black populations, ethnic and racial diversity, supportive relationships, nutrition and obesity. Other chapters present research, models, theories and procedures subjective to the well being of older Black citizens.

191. Jones, James H. *Bad Blood: The Tuskegee Syphilis Experiment*. New York: The Free Press, 1993. 297 pp., includes bibliography and index, hardcover $24.95, paperback $11.95. ISBN 0-029-16675-6. Jones documents the government experiment, known as the Tuskegee Experiment, with syphilis treatment from 1932 to 1972. During these years, government doctors infected and refused treatment for syphilis to four hundred poor, uneducated Black Alabama farmers. The inhumane study failed to provide conclusive medical data on the disease in Black patients. Jones connects the Tuskegee Experiment to contemporary Black American's distrust in national health organizations.

192. Jones, Woodrow, Jr. and Rice, Mitchell F. (eds.). *Health Care Issues in Black America: Policies, Problems and Prospects.* Westport, CT: Greenwood Press, 1987. 255 pp., includes bibliography and index, paperback $39.95. ISBN 0-313-24886-9. This collection edited by political scientists Jones and Rice focuses on the impact of institutional racism and economic inequality on the health of the American Black community. The authors see a lack of commitment by society towards health care for Blacks.

193. Lemelle, Anthony J., Jr. *Black Male Deviance.* Westport, CT: Praeger, 1995. 208 pp., includes index, hardcover $52.95. ISBN 0-275-95004-2. The author attempts to contribute to an understanding of the African-American male. Lemelle takes a less common approach by centering his work on the positives of Black men in America. The author explores Black male deviance through an Afrocentric perspective. In his sociological analysis, Lemelle argues that Black male deviance is a consequence both of oppression and Black males' fight against it.

194. Reed, James N. *The Black Man's Guide to Good Health: Essential Advice for the Special Concerns of African-American Men.* New York: Berkley Publishing, 1994. 288 pp., paperback $12.00. ISBN 0-399-52138-0. This book, which was researched by a team of experts in African-American healthcare, addresses every condition from sickle cell anemia to strokes.

195. Steward, James. "The Political Economy of Black Male Suicides," *Journal of Black Studies*, v 11, 1980, pp. 249-261. The author examines the increase in Black male suicide rates, and the connection between economic position and suicide. The author places blame for Black male suicide on both economics and societal treatment.

10

History and Social Life

196. Aldridge, Delores P. *Focusing: Black Male-Female Relationships.* Dubuque, IA: Kendall/Hunt Publishing Company, 1989. 235 pp., includes bibliography, paperback $8.95. ISBN 0-883-78140-9. This book deals with Black male/female relationships. Aldridge addresses the impact of interracial dating on Black relationships and explores demographic data related to Black men and women. She explores the role of sexism, the availability and economic status of Black males, marital relations, religion, and conflicts between Black men and women.

197. Allen, Robert L. and Boyd, Herbert (eds.). *Brotherman: The Odyssey of Black Men in America, An Anthology.* New York: Ballantine Books, 1995. Paperback $19.95. ISBN 0-345-38317-6. The 1995 winner of the American Book Award, this text explores the life experiences of Black men. More than 150 men contributed to this anthology of poems, stories, and excerpts from novels and autobiographies.

198. Anderson, Elijah. *A Place on the Corner.* Chicago: University of Chicago Press, 1978. 237 pp., includes bibliography and index, hardcover $15.95. ISBN 0-226-01953-5 (H), 0-226-01954-3 (P). Anderson studies the status systems of Chicago's ghettos. He particularly focuses on a bar called Jelly's, where he observed and interacted with Black men who socialized there. He addresses the rules and principles under which they participated, their social hierarchies, and their methods

of social interaction.   He describes in detail the informal social stratification system they created.

199. Andrews, William L. (ed.). *Critical Essays on Frederick Douglass.* Boston: G.K. Hall, 1991. 217 pp. $40.00. ISBN 0-816-17301-X. A volume of commentary and interpretation of Douglass's writings. Andrews' introduction maps Douglass's reputation as well as the substantive themes of the literary criticism.

200. Aptheker, Herbert.   *American Negro Slave Revolts.*   New York: International Publishers, 1983. 415 pp., includes bibliography and index, paperback $9.95. ISBN 0-717-80605-7. Aptheker gives an in-depth account of resistance to slavery. He writes about the efforts of Nat Turner, Denmark Vesey, and Gabriel Prosser, among others. The book provides information on the conditions which slaves lived under, what drove them to rebel, and the efforts that Whites took to combat these rebellions.

201. Aptheker, Herbert (ed.). *Nat Turner's Slave Rebellion.* New York: Humanities Press, 1966. 152 pp., includes bibliography. ISBN 0-391-02898-7. This is truly a detailed examination of the slave rebellion led by Nat Turner. The book includes the complete text of the original edition of Nat Turner's so-called "Confessions" of 1831. The book addresses the environment, economic depression, population disproportion, and Southampton County.

202. Baker-Fletcher, Garth. *Xodus: An African-American Male Journey.* Minneapolis, MN: Fortress Press, 1995. 198 pp., includes bibliography and index, paperback $17.00. ISBN 0-800-62918-3. This text aims at innovative, positive "reconstruction" of African-American maleness. The book examines the traditional, present, and future roles of Black men in their communities.

203. Barbeau, Arthur E. and Henri, Florette. *The Unknown Soldiers: African-American Troops in W.W.I.* New York: DaCapo Press, 1996. 279 pp., includes bibliography and index, paperback $14.95. ISBN 0-306-80694-0. In this book, Barbeau and Henri detail the experiences of Black soldiers during World War I. They address Black soldiers' ability to perform in the face of severe discrimination. They reveal the poor training, inferior equipment and substandard supplies Black troops were given. The authors also include details of physical and verbal harassment.

204. Belton, David. *Each Night I Die*. Edgewood, MD: M.E. Duncan & Company, Inc., 1992. 217 pp., paperback $12.95. ISBN 1-878-64707-5. This book is a compelling autobiography of the life of David Belton. He explores how he and his family survived the frightening conditions of poverty, violence, racism, poor education, and general hopelessness. In describing his own life, Belton evaluates many aspects of Black life. He distinctly focuses on Black men as well as the life of Black prisoners. The author investigates the criminal justice system in the United States and its administration in order to find better solutions to the problem of rising numbers of Black inmates.

205. Black, Daniel P. *Dismantling Black Manhood: An Historical and Literary Analysis of the Legacy of Slavery*. New York: Garland Publishers, 1997. 190 pp., includes bibliography and index, $39.00. ISBN 0-815-32857-5. Based on documents covering the period 1794-1863. Black shows how symbols of manhood in pre-colonial West Africa were destroyed by the institution of slavery. He goes on to describe how captivity erased their roles as warrior, father, and protector. He also shows how men fulfilled these symbols through such aspects like sexual prowess and household domination.

206. Blount, Marcellus and Cunningham, George P. *Representing Black Men*. New York: Routledge, 1996. 236 pp., includes bibliography and index, hardcover $55.00, paperback $17.95. ISBN 0-415-97058-6 (H), 0-415-90759-4 (P). With essays written by eminent scholars and critics, this book explores the position of African-American men in American society. Grouped under three sections, "Against Patriarchy," "Negotiating Masculinity," and "Screening Men", the essays examine how Black males are portrayed through the media, literature, society and culture. Issues such as masculinity, racism and sexuality and how the Black male copes with these are examined in the various essays.

207. Bolster, William Jeffrey. *Black Jacks: African-American Seamen in the Age of Sail*. Cambridge, MA: Harvard University Press, 1997. 360 pp., includes index, hardcover $27.00, paperback $14.95. ISBN 0-674-07624-9 (H), 0-674-07627-3 (P). Bolster writes how Black sailors (free Blacks and slaves) helped to shape the naval force during the period 1740-1860 and the various roles Blacks served on these naval ships. Bolster examines the relationships between Blacks and Whites on the ships, in port, and the English POW camp of Dartmoor.

208. Boyd, Herb and Allen, Robert L. (eds.). *Brotherman: The Odyssey of Black Men in America, An Anthology*. New York: Ballantine Books,

1995. 910 pp., includes bibliography, hardcover $35.00, paperback $19.95. ISBN 0-345-37670-6 (H), 0-345-38317-6 (P). This anthology combines numerous pieces of Black male literature ranging from slave narratives to poems and writings by men such as Malcolm X. It demonstrates the rich diversity of this literature and the positive contribution Black men have made to American culture.

209. Boykin, Keith. *One More River to Cross: Black and Gay in America.* New York: Anchor Press. 272 pp., hardcover $23.95. ISBN 0-385-47982-4. Boykin, a gay Black man, Harvard Law School graduate, and political activist offers a personal exploration, in a political tone, of the Black and gay communities. Boykin explores the gay lifestyle from the African-American male perspective and stresses the need for civil rights laws to include gays and lesbians in their protection.

210. Bradden, W.S. *Under Three Banners: An Autobiography.* Nashville, TN: National Baptist Publishing Board, 1940. 287 pp., includes index. This book is about a man who was a minister, a soldier, and someone who has seen the entire world. In this book he discusses dangers he was involved in, near-death escapes, hardships, and bitter disappointments. The book is not intended for circulation but rather to stay within the Berean church (of which Bradden was a minister) and passed on to the children thereof. The book also discusses the role the Berean church played in WWI and gives accounts written during the war.

211. Brown, William W. *The Negro in the American Rebellion: His Heroism and His Fidelity.* New York: Mnemosyne Publishing Co., 1997. Originally published in 1867 by Lee and Shepard. 380 pp., paperback $15.00. ISBN 1-566-75003-2. The book was first written in 1867 as an attempt by William Wells Brown to present an account of the role of Blacks in suppressing the slaveholders' rebellion. The book is based on primary evidence and first hand accounts of events of the time, and serves to highlight the particularly active and brave role undertaken by Black men in the Civil War. Brown also covers the role of Black soldiers in the War for Independence and the War of 1812.

212. Cleage, Pearl. *Deals With the Devil and Other Reasons to Riot.* New York: Ballantine Books, 1994. 304 pp., hardcover $22.00, paperback $11.00. ISBN 0-345-38278-1 (H), 0-345-38871-2 (P). Cleage, a columnist for the *Atlanta Tribune,* editor of *Catalyst* magazine, and both a feminist and Black nationalist, offers 40 lively essays on a wide range of topics. Among the topics included are Clarence Thomas, Malcolm X and Cleage's reflections on love, marriage, and friends.

213. Costanzo, Angelo. *Surprising Narrative: Olaudah Equiano and the Beginnings of Black Autobiography.* Westport, CT: Greenwood Press, 1987. 149 pp., includes bibliography and index, hardcover $29.95. ISBN 0-313-25633-0. Olaudah Equiano's autobiography was very influential when first published, and is still used in many college classrooms. Costanzo explores the conflict between Equiano's profession that his work is antislavery and his belief that the system of slavery, rather than slaveholders themselves, was responsible for the evil of human bondage.

214. Davis, Benjamin O., Jr. *Benjamin O. Davis, Jr., American: An Autobiography.* Washington, DC: Smithsonian Institution Press, 1991. 442 pp., includes index, $19.95. ISBN 0-874-74742-2. Davis retired as a three-star general from the Air Force in 1970 after commanding the integrated 51st Fighter Wing in Korea and the 13th Air Force during Vietnam and leading the all-Black 99th Fighter Squadron in WWII. Davis, the first Black this century to graduate from West Point, has held numerous civilian post positions. This is primarily the story of Davis' struggle to be a leader within the armed services as a Black man.

215. Dawsey, Darrell. *Living To Tell About It: Young Black Men in America Speak Their Piece.* Anchor: Doubleday, 1996. 368 pp., $22.95. ISBN 0-385-47313-3. The author visited nine cities and interviewed Black men between the ages of 15 and 24 for this book. Issues covered include work, childhood, violence, parent/child relationships, spirituality, and respect. The book shatters myths about young Black men as it explores their life experiences. The blame for struggles faced by young Black men is placed primarily with the White power structure.

216. Douglass, Frederick, edited by Andrews, William L. *My Bondage and My Freedom.* Urbana: University of Illinois Press, 1988 (originally published 1855). 307 pp., includes index, hardcover $37.95. ISBN 0-405-01813-4 (H), 0-252-01410-3 (P). This autobiography of Frederick Douglass covers his life from 1817 to 1855. It focuses mainly on Black struggles Douglass witnessed during his lifetime. He writes a biography of the abolitionist movement, the Black slave, and the fugitive slave. He highlights conditions within slavery, commenting on plantation life in Maryland from a 19th century perspective.

217. Drake, St. Clair and Cayton, Horace R. *Black Metropolis: A Study of Negro Life in a Northern City.* Chicago: University of Chicago Press, 1993 (revised and enlarged edition). 858 pp., includes bibliography. ISBN 0-226-16234-6. Drake and Cayton's thoroughly researched book focuses on the economic, political, social, and cultural aspects of Black

life in Chicago up to 1960. The text remains one of the best studies on American urbanization.

218. Dryden, Charles W. *A-Train: Memoirs of a Tuskegee Airman.* Tuscaloosa: University of Alabama Press, 1997. 421 pp., includes bibliography and index, hardcover $29.95. ISBN 0-817-30856-3. As a member of the first group of African-Americans to be trained as military pilots during W.W.II, Dryden had to overcome enormous obstacles to serve his country. The pilots trained at Tuskegee overcame grave stereotypes and had a distinguished record. Squadrons slatted by Tuskegee airmen never lost a bomber escort. Dryden details the obstacles and discrimination these men confronted.

219. Duberman, Martin B. *Paul Robeson.* New York: The New Press, 1995. 804 pp., includes bibliography and index, $19.95. ISBN 0-394-52780-1. Duberman thorough research includes use of Robeson's personal files as well as FBI files to provide rich detail. Duberman covers Robeson's many roles in life: actor, concert hall singer, lawyer, academician, linguist, political revolutionary and communist.

220. DuBois, W.E.B. *Black Reconstruction in America.* New York: Atheneum, 1992. Originally published under title *Black Reconstruction* by New York: Harcourt Brace in 1935. Includes bibliography and index, paperback $18.00. ISBN 0-689-70063-6. W.E.B. DuBois addresses the role of Blacks in the post-Civil War reconstruction era in the United States. DuBois sees reconstruction as a tragic story of class struggle and places the blame for the failure of reconstruction largely upon White labor that regularly failed to rescue their Black counterparts. DuBois contradicts the popular myth that Blacks dominated reconstruction.

221. Duneier, Mitchell. *Slim's Table: Race, Respectability, and Masculinity.* Chicago: University of Chicago Press, 1992. 192 pp., includes bibliography and index, hardcover $19.95, paperback $9.95. ISBN 0-226-17030-6 (H), 0-226-17031-4 (P). Duneier provides an ethnography of a South Side Chicago community, from a participant-observation position. Duneier focuses on the "regulars" at Valois cafeteria, mostly Black men, and provides detailed portraits of these men and their interactions. He argues that the men share self-control, respectability, and sociability and that these qualities are reinforced by their interactions.

222. Elkins, Stanley M. *Slavery: A Problem in American Institutional and Intellectual Life.* Chicago: University of Chicago Press, 1976. 320 pp., includes bibliography and index, paperback $14.95. IBSN 0-226-20477-

4 (P). This book discusses the institution of slavery and its continuing effects on the Black community and family. Elkins argues that slavery impacts contemporary political, social, and economic conditions. He observes slavery as an institution and slavery's effect on the personality and social life of both White and Black people.

223. Flipper, Henry O. with Harris, Theodore D. *Black Frontiersman: The Memoirs of Henry O. Flipper, First Black Graduate of West Point.* Fort Worth, TX: Texas Christian University Press, 1997. 196 pp., includes bibliography and index, paperback $22.95. ISBN 0-875-65171-2. This book traces Flipper's career to his retirement and death at his brother's Atlanta home in 1940. In 1877, Henry Flipper became the first Black graduate of the United States Military Academy. He later became the first Black commissioned officer in the Regular Army. After his dismissal from the Army in 1882, Flipper pursued a career as a mining engineer and surveyor. He also wrote a monograph on the Black explorer Estevanico.

224. Folsom, Franklin. *The Life and Legend of George McJunkin: Black Cowboy.* New York: Nelson, 1973. 162 pp. ISBN 0-840-76326-3. This biography of McJunkin, a Black cowboy, follows his career from the 1860s to the 1920s. Folsom carries the reader through McJunkin's travels in Colorado, Texas, and New Mexico.

225. Franklin, John Hope. *George Washington Williams: A Biography.* Durham, NC: Duke University Press, 1998. 400 pp., paperback $18.95. ISBN 0-822-32164-5 (P). In this biography of George Washington Williams, Franklin examines the man and his times. He argues that Williams' continuing legacy is based on his commitment to "the dignity as well as the rights of darker peoples everywhere." Franklin concludes that Williams was ultimately unhappy and unfulfilled.

226. Gary, Lawrence E. (ed.). *Black Men.* Newbury Park, CA: Sage Publications, 1981. 295 pp., includes bibliography and index, $21.95. ISBN 0-803-91655-8. This book, divided into four sections, is a collection of articles on major issues affecting the status and behavior of Black men in America. These issues include the social and health status of Black men, their involvement in family life, their psychological and social coping patterns, and Black men's interactions with various social institutions. This book gives a fairly comprehensive look at the position of Black men in America, and how their position may be improved.

227. Gary, Lawrence E. and Leashore, Bogart R. "The High Risk Status of Black Men," *Social Work*, v 27, 1982, pp. 54-58. While many studies are

completed on Black society, most are focused on women and children rather than Black men. The basic premise of this study is that institutional racism is responsible for the vulnerability of Black men. The study focuses on the injustices Black men have suffered rather than advantages they have in society. The authors state several myths about Black men and explore common stereotypes such as the Sambo of the nineteenth century.

228. Gates, Henry Louis, Jr. *Thirteen Ways Of Looking at a Black Man.* New York: Random House, 1997. 224 pp., $21.00. ISBN 0-679-45713-5. Gates, the head of Harvard's Afro-American Studies program, is one of the leading contemporary Black scholars. Originally published in the New Yorker, Gates offers here a collection of detailed portraits of prominent Black men including literary critic Albert Murray, choreographer Bill T. Jones, singer/activist Harry Belafonte, retired General Colin Powell, Nation of Islam leader Louis Farrakhan, and New York Times literary critic Anatole Broyard. Gates also includes an essay on Black responses to the O.J. Simpson trial.

229. Gibbs, Jewelle Taylor (ed.). *Young, Black, and Male in America: An Endangered Species.* Dover, MA: Auburn House Publishing Co., 1988. 377 pp., hardcover $28.95, paperback $17.95. ISBN 0-865-69180-0 (P). In this study, social scientists and experts analyze the deteriorating status of Black males. They discuss demographics, as well as economic, political, and sociocultural issues. Issues such as substance abuse, teen pregnancy, and crime and delinquency are examined. The authors argue that we need to develop programs and policies that attack the underlying social and structural factors impacting Black male youth, and create a comprehensive family policy and network of services that address the problems of Black youth.

230. Gilder, George. *Visible Man: A True Story of Post-Racist America.* 1995. 240 pp., paperback $16.95. ISBN 1-55815-465-5. This volume, originally published in 1979, tells the story of Sam Brewer, a young African-American man unjustly accused of rape. Though the book focuses on Brewer, the circumstances surrounding the accusations brought against him paint a larger picture of the obstacles faced by Black youth in America. As few of these obstacles have been removed since 1979, the book is still timely.

231. Grier, William H. and Cobbs, Price. M. *Black Rage.* New York: Basic Books, 1992. 256 pp., paperback $14.00. ISBN 0-465-00701-5 (P). Grier and Cobbs, both Black psychiatrists, describe the plight of African-

Americans from slavery to the present. The authors provide a clear and concise account of family life, womanhood, manhood, education and employment.

232. Hair, William Ivy. *Carnival of Fury: Robert Charles and the New Orleans Race Riot of 1900*. Baton Rouge: Louisiana State University Press, 1986. 216 pp., paperback $11.95. ISBN 0-871-13484. Thoroughly researched, this book is an account of the New Orleans race riot of 1900. The main focus of the book is Robert Charles, a black laborer who drew national attention when he shot twenty-seven Whites, seven of whom were policemen. Virtually unknown before the incident, Charles became an instant hero to some Blacks and a source of fear for Whites.

233. Harlan, Louis R. *Booker T. Washington: The Wizard of Tuskegee, 1901-1915*. New York: Oxford University Press, 1983. 548 pp., includes bibliography and index, hardcover $30.00, paperback $16.95. ISBN 0-195-03202-0 (H), 0-195-04229-8 (P). This book is about a man Harlan describes as "complex, devious, and authoritarian...who continued to be the accommodationist, political boss, and secret opponent of White supremacy." Harlan details Booker T. Washington's support of Howard and Fisk Universities as he describes Washington's political power.

234. Harris, Trudier. *Exorcising Blackness: Historical and Literary Lynching and Burning Rituals*. Bloomington, Indiana: Indiana University Press, 1984. 222 pp., includes bibliography and index, $22.50. ISBN 0-253-31995-1. Harris attempts to explain the use of lynchings, castration, rape and Black mutilation by authors such as Paul Laurence Dunbar, Sutton Griggs, Ralph Ellison, Langston Hughes, and others. Harris probes the recurrent theme of physical threat and fear in Black male writers' works. The author also explores authors' attempts to illuminate racism by writing about blatantly racist actions.

235. Hawkins, Walter L. *African-American Generals and Flag Officers: Biographies of Over 120 Blacks in the United States Military*. Jefferson, NC: McFarland & Company, 1993. 264 pp., includes index, hardcover $29.95. ISBN 0-899-50774-3. Hawkins provides short illustrated biographies of the 119 Blacks who have risen to the rank of general or its equivalent since Benjamin O. Davis, Sr. was the first Black to attain that rank in 1940. Each biography gives an account of the subjects' birth, family, and education.

236. Hemphill, Essex (ed.). *Brother to Brother: New Writings by Black Gay Men.* Boston, MA: Alyson Publications, 1991. 274 pp., includes bibliography, paperback $10.95. ISBN 1-555-83146-X. Hemphill explores the lives of gay Black males in America. The book offers many different subjects that include collections of stories about gay Black men. It also provides biographical information on the various authors. The book gives insight into what it is like to be Black and gay in America.

237. Hersey, John. *The Algiers Motel Incident.* Baltimore, MD: Johns Hopkins University Press, 1997. 397 pp., paperback $15.95. ISBN 0-801-85777-5. The author interviewed participants and examined police and court evidence concerning the event that took place on the fourth day of the Detroit riots, when police snipers killed three African-Americans. This is derived from research that explains the atmosphere and consequences of the events that took place at the Algiers Motel.

238. Hill, Robert and Bair, Barbara (eds.). *Marcus Garvey: Life and Lessons.* Berkeley: University of California Press, 1987. 451 pp., includes bibliography, hardcover $25.00, paperback $16.95. ISBN 0-520-06214-0 (H), 0-520-06265-5 (P). This book is a collection of speeches and writings by Marcus Garvey (1887-1940). Garvey gained fame in the U.S. with his influence in the Universal Negro Improvement Association. The book also has a significant introduction that discusses Garvey's significance and his theories.

239. hooks, bell. *Black Looks: Race and Representation.* Boston, MA: South End Press, 1992. 200 pp., includes bibliography, paperback $12.00, hardcover $30.00. ISBN 0-896-08433-7 (P). Throughout this book, hooks discusses issues of racism, sexism, and multiculturalism. She does this by explaining how different races are represented to one another. She asks the reader to challenge the negative images of Black people that reinforce the idea of White supremacy. This book offers a refreshing approach to confronting the monotonous problems of racism and sexism.

240. Horowitz, Helen Lefkowitz and Peiss, Kathy (eds.). *Love Across the Color Line: The Letters of Alice Hanley to Channing Lewis.* Amherst, MA: University of Massachusetts Press, 1996. 144 pp., includes bibliography, hardcover $35.00, paperback $13.95. ISBN 1-558-49023-X (H), 1-558-49024-8 (P). This book begins in 1992 with the story of a couple in Northampton, MA, who find a bundle of letters in their attic. The letters they found are from a White working-class woman by the name of Alice Hanley to her African-American lover, Channing Lewis. Hanley and her family had lived in the house eighty years earlier. This

book contains the twenty-seven letters written from 1907 to 1908 and describes their interracial relationship.

241. Jefferson, Paul. *The Travels of William Wells Brown, including The Narrative of William Wells Brown, a fugitive slave, and The American Fugitive in Europe, sketches of places and people abroad.* New York: Markus Wiener Publications, 1991. 235 pp., includes bibliography, paperback $14.95. ISBN 1-558-76042-3 (H), 1-558-76043-1 (P). Brown was a runaway slave turned abolitionist. The current volume combines his two best-known works. The first, published in 1847, deals with the author's life in slavery and his escape to freedom in the North. The second details the author's travels in Europe in the early 1850s, where he was sent to lobby support for the abolitionist cause.

242. Jordan, Winthrop D. *White Over Black: American Attitudes toward the Negro, 1550-1812.* Baltimore, Maryland: Penguin Books, 1969. 615 pp., includes bibliography, hardcover $50.00, paperback $18.95. ISBN 0-807-81055-X (H), 0-807-84550-7 (P). This book examines the role of the African-American in moral and intellectual terms. Jordan explores the periods of American settlement, expansion, revolution, and independence.

243. Kaplan, Sidney. *The Black Presence in the Era of the American Revolution, 1770-1800.* Boston, MA: University of Massachusetts Press, 1989. 241 pp., includes index, paperback $18.95. ISBN 0-870-23662-8 (H), 0-870-23663-6 (P). Kaplan uses more than 100 reproductions of portraits and facsimiles of letters, diaries, and other documents to demonstrate the role of Blacks in the American Revolution. He includes people such as Benjamin Banneker and Olaudah Equiano as well as many others.

244. Lamar, Jake. *Bourgeois Blues: An American Memoir.* New York: Summit Books, 1991. 174 pp., hardcover $20.00, paperback $10.95. ISBN 0-671-69191-0 (H), 0-452-26911-3 (P). This autobiography traces Lamar's life as a child in a middle-class family with an abusive father. The setting is New York in the 1960s and 70s, and Lamar discusses dysfunctional families. He explores the Black middle-class struggle to assimilate into White society while maintaining acceptance in the Black community.

245. Liebow, Elliot. *Tally's Corner: A Study of Negro Street Corner Men.* Boston, MA: Little, Brown and Co., 1999. 288 pp., paperback $12.95. ISBN 0-316-55809-5. Liebow describes Black family life in inner-city Washington, DC. The main themes of the book are Black culture,

poverty, and oppression. Liebow discusses the fact that these conditions are very difficult to survive in, much less thrive in.

246. Litwack, Leon F. *Been in the Storm so Long: The Aftermath of Slavery.* New York: Random House, 1979. 651 pp., includes bibliography and index, paperback $20.00. ISBN 0-394-50099-7 (H), 0-394-74398-9 (P). Litwack's book is about the years leading to 1867 when Radical Reconstruction was about to be fully launched. He tells much about White people's responses to the end of slavery. However, Litwack primarily focuses on the ways in which freedom was perceived and experienced by Black men and women born into slavery and how they acted to help shape their future as freedmen and freedwomen.

247. Love, Nat. *The Life and Adventures of Nat Love.* Lincoln: University of Nebraska Press, 1995. 162 pp., paperback $9.00. ISBN 0-803-27955-8. Love's autobiography tells his experiences after the Civil War. His story is filled with exciting and nearly unbelievable instances of courage. His narrative is boastful and full of confrontations with frontier dangers.

248. Lusane, Clarence. *Pipe Dream Blues: Racism and the War on Drugs.* Boston: South End Press, 1991. 234 pp., includes bibliography and index, hardcover $30.00, paperback $12.00. ISBN 0-089-60841-6 (H), 0-896-08410-8 (P). Lusane examines the history of the drug trade and drug abuse in the United States. He analyzes Washington's drug culture, as well as the social, economic and political impact of the war on drugs on people of color. He offers a number of strategies to fight drug trafficking and highlights the importance of political and economic power.

249. Lyles, Charlise. *Do I Dare Disturb the Universe?: From the Projects to Prep School.* Boston, MA: Faber and Faber, Inc., 1994. 226 pp., includes bibliography, hardcover $21.95. ISBN 0-571-19836-8. A compelling memoir of the struggles and ambition of a young African-American from a Cleveland housing project.

250. Lynn, Conrad J. and Kunstler, William M. *There Is a Fountain: The Autobiography of Conrad Lynn.* Brooklyn, NY: Lawrence Hill Books, 1993. 268 pp., hardcover $27.00, paperback $11.95. ISBN 1-556-52165-0 (H), 1-556-52166-9. This is an autobiography of a successful African-American activist attorney. Lynn had a full life and although the book contains some personal information, it primarily focuses on the cases he fought. The trial stories are inspiring, and Lynn recalls his action-filled, remarkable life with modesty and candor.

251. Manning, Kenneth R. *Black Apollo of Science: The Life of Ernest Everett Just.* New York: Oxford University Press, 1983. 397 pp., includes bibliography and index, hardcover $29.95, paperback $13.95. ISBN 0-195-03299-3 (H), 0-195-03498-8 (P). Manning has written the first biography of Everett Just, more than one hundred years after the noted scientist died. Manning's research includes many interviews with Just, and he gives a detailed look at the life of a man who made enormous contributions to marine biology despite major obstacles.

252. McCall, Nathan. *Makes Me Wanna Holler: A Young Black Man in America.* New York: Random House, 1994. 404 pp., hardcover $23.00. ISBN 0-679-41268-9 (H), 0-679-74070-8 (P). In the same genre as Richard Wright's *Native Son* (1939), this book chronicles the author's life. The author gives an account of what it is really like to be a young Black man in America. Shunning middle-class affluence for a life of crime, McCall spent more than three years in prison. While in prison, he learned how to salvage his life. This account is largely a story of transformation and triumph, as McCall ultimately became a journalist for the *Washington Post.*

253. McFeely, William S. *Frederick Douglass.* New York: Norton, 1991. 465 pp., includes bibliography and index, hardcover $24.95, paperback $14.95. ISBN 0-393-02823-2 (H), 0-393-31376-X (P). This is a Pulitzer-Prize winning biography of Douglass. McFeely makes a connection between Douglass and Benjamin Franklin, noting that they were both in a "lifelong process of inventing themselves." However, unlike Franklin, Douglass received little recognition or political power during his lifetime.

254. McGuire, Phillip. *He, too, Spoke for Democracy: Judge Hastie, W.W.II, and the Black Soldier.* Westport, CT: Greenwood Press, 1988. 154 pp., includes bibliography and index. ISBN 0-313-26115-6. A detailed account of Judge Hastie's role as a civilian aide in the War Department during the first two years of WWII. This text graphically reveals the harshness of the racially segregated US Army. McGuire details Hastie's efforts to bring about change, the determination of Army leadership to remain segregated, and the Army's blatant institutional racism. Hastie's work started the move toward the eventual abolition of military segregation.

255. Meeks, Cordell D. *To Heaven through Hell: An Autobiography of the First Black District Judge of Kansas.* Kansas City, KS: Corcell Publishers, 1986. 242 pp. Cordell Meeks tells his long struggle to become the first Black district judge in Kansas. In this autobiography, he

tells how he gained his position through trust and determination to override stereotypes. He also tells of the joy he had in being elected the first Black district court judge in Kansas.

256. Moses, Wilson J. *Alexander Crummell: A Study of Civilization and Discontent*. New York: Oxford University Press, 1992. 400 pp., paperback $35.00. ISBN 0-870-23796-9. This is a reprint of W.E.B. DuBois's "Of Alexander Crummell," and a collection of Crummell's letters, reports, sermons, and articles. Crummell was a priest, scholar, and founder of the American Negro Academy. This biography covers his years in Liberia and his establishment and pastorship of St. Luke's Episcopal Church in Washington, DC. It also includes his last years writing, lecturing and challenging the racial leadership of Booker T. Washington.

257. Oates, Stephen B. *The Fires of Jubilee: Nat Turner's Fierce Rebellion*. New York: HarperCollins, 1990. 208 pp., paperback $13.00. ISBN 0-060-91670-2. A vivid retelling of Nat Turner's insurrection, the most famous slave revolt in the history of American slavery.

258. Okwu, Julian C.R. *Face Forward: Young African-American Men in a Critical Age*. San Francisco: Chronicle, 1997. Hardcover $35.00, paperback $19.95. ISBN 0-8118-1631-1 (H), 0-8118-1215-4 (P). In a collection of photos and mini-profiles, Okwu provides a platform for 40 young African-Americans. Their lives challenge media images and stereotypes of young Black men as being involved solely in rap, sports, and crime.

259. Page, Clarence. *Showing My Color: Impolite Essays on Race and Identity*. New York: Harper Collins Publishers, 1996. 306 pp., includes bibliography, paperback $15.00. ISBN 0-694-51647-3 (H), 0-060-92801-8 (P). Drawing on personal experiences, this series of original essays covers the central questions of gender, race, and ethnic identity. Page attempts to show what it means to be Black in America. He explores subjects such as "integration fatigue," the Colin Powell phenomenon, and more.

260. Painter, Nell Irvin. *Exodusters: Black Migration to Kansas after Reconstruction*. New York: Alfred A. Knopf, 1977. 288 pp., includes bibliography and index, paperback $10.95. ISBN 0-394-40253-7 (H), 0-393-00951-3 (P). In this book, Painter gives a detailed account of the political, social, and economic reasons for Southern Black migration to Kansas in the late 1870s and 1880s. In particular, Painter sites the

influence of Henry Adams and Benjamin "Pap" Singleton in leading
Blacks to the Midwest.

261. Phelps, J. Alfred. *Chappie: America's First Black Four-Star: The Life
and Times of Daniel James, Jr.* Novato, CA: Presidio Press, 1991. 366
pp., includes bibliography and index, paperback $9.95. ISBN 0-891-
41464-9. This popular biography describes the man who reached the
controversial role as spokesman for America's Vietnam policies. Daniel
James regarded himself as an Air Force officer who was Black, rather
than a Black Air Force officer. This is a well-written account of General
James' professional life and personal relationships.

262. Phelps, J. Alfred. *They Had a Dream: The Story of African-American
Astronauts.* Novato, CA: Presidio Press, 1994. 291 pp., includes
bibliography and index, paperback $24.95. ISBN 0-891-41497-5. An Air
Force veteran and author, Phelps has crafted a readable series of essays.
Phelps uses interviews and other sources to tell the stories of among
others Ron McNair, one of the crew who died in the Challenger accident,
Edward Dwight, who was eventually denied astronaut status, and Robert
Lawrence, who died in a controversial flying accident.

263. Pickens, William, edited by Andrews, William L. *Bursting Bonds:
Enlarged Edition [of] The Heir of Slaves: Autobiography of a "New
Negro."* Bloomington: Indiana University Press, 1991. 76 pp., includes
bibliography, hardcover $25.00. ISBN 0-253-34496-4. This book tells
the life of William Pickens (1881-1954) who was the sixth of ten children
of former slaves. A Phi Beta Kappa graduate of Yale University, Pickens
achieved much recognition as a prominent Black leader. The text draws
an outline of Black experiences from 1877 to 1964. Among other things,
Pickens covers the creation and early life of the NAACP and traces race
relations in this period.

264. Powell, Colin L. with Persico, Joseph E. *My American Journey.* New
York: Random House, 1995. 643 pp., includes index, paperback $25.95.
ISBN 0-679-43296-5 (H), 0-679-76511-5 (P). This is an autobiography
of General Colin Powell, the first Black Chairman of the Joint Chiefs of
Staff. This personable well-written book details Powell's rules for running
a meeting, his political philosophy, and experiences such as getting
caught by Pentagon security with an antique rifle.

265. Rawick, George P. *The American Slave: A Composite Autobiography.*
Westport, CT: Greenwood Press, 1972. (Fourteen separate volumes.)
This is a collection of slave narratives consisting of interviews with ex-

slaves in the 1930s, and the Fisk University slave narrative collection, compiled from interviews with former slaves in the 1920s. The narratives are reprinted in their entirety, free of editing.

266. Redkey, Edwin. *Black Exodus: Black Nationalist and Back-to-Africa Movements, 1890-1910*. New Haven, CT: Yale University Press, 1969. 319 pp., paperback $10.00. ISBN 0-300-01138-5. Redkey explores the relationship between Black nationalist sentiment and the desire of many American Blacks to return to Africa in order to escape injustice, poverty, and discrimination.

267. Roth, David. *Sacred Honor: Colin Powell, The Inside Account of His Life and Triumphs*. New York: Harper Collins, 1994. 272 pp., paperback $6.50. ISBN 0-061-00849-4. This book is an intimate portrait of the man who went from Harlem to the White House to the forefront of Operation Desert Storm. Based on extensive research, this insider's biography reveals the complete Colin Powell.

268. Rutledge, Aaron L. and Gass, Gertrude Zemon. *Nineteen Negro Men--Personality and Manpower Retraining*. San Francisco: Jossey-Bass Inc., 1967. 109 pp., includes index, hardcover $65.00. ISBN 0-835-79341-9. This book gives a brief report of an in-depth study on nineteen Black men who had never held long-term jobs. The men, representative of the unemployed in Detroit at the time, entered a retraining program for practical nurses at the Shapero School of Nursing at Sinai Hospital in Detroit. Rutledge and Gass address the main issues covered in the study as well as the results and recommendations.

269. Smith, Michael J. (ed.). *Black Men-White Men: A Gay Anthology*. San Francisco: Gay Sunshine Press, 1983. 238 pp., includes bibliography. ISBN 0-917-34227-5. This book is a collaboration of short stories, poems, drawings, and testimonies from Black and White gay men in the United States. It addresses issues such as racism in the media, the Black church response, and coming out.

270. Sochen, June. *The Black Man and the American Dream: Negro Aspirations in America, 1900-1930*. Chicago: Quadrangle Books, 1971. 373 pp. ISBN 0-812-90161-4. This is a collection of articles from periodicals written primarily by Blacks. It is divided into four parts: The American Dream, The American Nightmare, The Irony of the Dream, and Other Dreams.

271. Sprague, Stuart Seely (ed.). *His Promised Land: The Autobiography of John P. Parker Former Slave and Conductor on the Underground Railroad*. New York: W.W. Norton & Company, 1996. 165 pp., includes bibliography and index, hardcover $20.00, paperback $10.00. ISBN 0-393-03941-2 (H), 0-393-31718-8 (P). This text chronicles the life of John P. Parker. A Virginia slave, Parker survived the institution and dedicated his life to helping other slaves find freedom through the Underground Railroad. Parker captures the struggles, hopes, pain, and joy of slaves.

272. Stephens, George E., and Yacovone, Donald (ed.). *A Voice of Thunder: The Civil War Letters of George E. Stephens*. Chicago: University of Illinois Press, 1997. 350 pp., includes bibliography and index, hardcover $26.95. ISBN 0-252-02245-9. A Black reporter for the weekly *Anglo-African*, Stephens critiques the injustices he and fellow Black soldiers encountered while fighting the Civil War. Donald Yacovone edits the book and gives a detailed background of Stephens as a reporter, soldier, and Black man.

273. Tarpley, Natasha (ed.). *Testimony: Young African-Americans on Self-Discovery and Black Identity*. Boston: Beacon Press, 1995. 304 pp., hardcover $40.00, paperback $14.00. ISBN 0-8070-0928-8 (H), 0-8070-0929-6 (P). A collection of poetry and essays by young Black writers on subjects political, personal, and cultural. Grievances about prejudice, inequality, and ghetto pain dominate as topics range from family, love, and friends to art and aesthetics.

274. Terrell, John U. *Estevanico the Black*. Los Angeles: Westernlore Press Publishers, 1968. 155 pp., includes bibliography. This book is about the exploration of the American Southwest in 1539 by a Negro slave named Estevanico the Black. It is a carefully written study of Estevanico and his achievements. Terrell has a unique writing style that adds to the well-documented historical events.

275. Terry, Wallace (ed.). *Bloods: An Oral History of the Vietnam War by Black Veterans*. New York: Random House, 1992. 311 pp., includes index, paperback $5.95. ISBN 0-345-37666-8. Wallace Terry, a correspondent in Saigon for *Time Magazine* during the late 1960s, compiles the narratives of 20 Black Vietnam veterans from every level and branch of the military. Through his experiences while covering the war, the author discovered that Black men carried unique burdens during and after the war that their White counterparts did not.

276. Valentine, Bettylou. *Hustling and Other Hard Work: Lifestyles in the Ghetto*. New York: The Free Press, 1978. 183 pp., includes bibliography and index, $12.95. ISBN 0-029-33060-2 (H), 0-029-33070-X (P). Based on Valentine's five-year period of living in the ghetto among its residents, this text is divided into three sections to demonstrate the connection between work, welfare, and "hustling." Valentine shows the day to day survival among low-income minority residents and how they maintain cultural, social, and family relationships.

277. Vanzant, Iyanla. *The Spirit of a Man: A Vision of Transformation for Black Men and the Women Who Love Them*. San Francisco: Harper San Francisco, 1996. 278 pp., includes bibliography, hardcover $20.00, paperback $12.00. ISBN 0-06-251236-6 (H), 0-06-251239-0 (P). Vanzant uses ancient African spirituality, contemporary faith and self-knowledge to encourage Black men to be positive against the struggles they face in today's society. She wants them to recognize the energy of their own spirits, and to work towards rewarding relationships with each other and the women in their lives.

278. Washington, Booker T. *Up From Slavery*. New York: Penguin Books, 1986. 332 pp., includes index, paperback $9.95. ISBN 0-140-39051-0. Born into slavery, Washington struggled to receive an education. He became a leader who carefully balanced the demands of Blacks and the constraints imposed by Whites. Washington founded the Tuskegee Institute and had political influence. He advocated education, industriousness, and self-reliance.

279. Wesley, Charles H. *The History of Alpha Phi Alpha: A Development in Negro College Life*. Washington DC: The Foundation Publishers, 1948. 464 pp. Wesley charts the development of this early Black fraternity from its origin in 1905 until just after the Second World War. He covers the influence of WWI and WWII as well as the Depression on the fraternity's development. Wesley demonstrates the importance of Alpha Phi Alpha in the development of African-American education.

280. Wharton, Vernon L. *The Negro in Mississippi, 1865-1890*. Westport, CT: Greenwood Press, 1984. 298 pp., paperback $30.95. ISBN 0-313-24568-1. This book is a study of the reconstruction period in Mississippi. It tells how the Black race has dealt with the trials and tribulations throughout the years. The author details the struggle that occurred and gives examples of how people dealt with these issues.

281. White, Walter. *Rope and Faggot: A Biography of Judge Lynch.* New York: Ayer Company Publishers, 1978. 272 pp., includes bibliographic references. ISBN 0-405-01907-6 (H). Walter White, a great anti-lynching crusader of the 20th century, reports information he found while investigating lynchings for the NAACP as the Assistant Secretary in 1918. With light skin and blue eyes, White was able to penetrate "White" society and collect information from participants and observers of lynchings.

282. Wideman, Daniel J. and Preston, Rohan B. (eds.) (intro by Henry Louis Gates, Jr.). *Soulfires: Young Black Men on Love and Violence.* New York: Penguin Books, 1996. 406 pp., paperback, $13.95. ISBN 0-14-024275-5. Wideman and Preston present a diverse collection of poems, essays, drama and stories designed to give voice to the Black men and written mostly by unknown journalists, poets, novelists, professors, and students. Together, they cover major issues facing Black men today. These issues include Black-on-Black crime, the plight of Black men in prison, the level of violence in society, and the men's relationships with their fathers as well as with Black women.

283. Wilkins, Roger. *A Man's Life: An Autobiography.* New York: Oxford Bow Press, 1991. 384 pp., paperback $15.95. ISBN 0-918-02483-8. This text is a chronicle of the difficulties of a Black man to succeed in American society.

284. Williams, Gregory Howard. *Life on the Color Line: The True Story of a White Boy Who Discovered He was Black.* New York: Dutton, 1995. 285 pp. ISBN 0-525-93850-5. Williams, born around World War II, was the son of a White mother and a biracial father who passed for White. Williams skillfully illuminates the color line in this autobiography. After his parents' separation, Williams moves to his father's hometown, where everyone considers him Black. We see in vivid detail how his life greatly changed when he became a "Black" child.

285. Wingfield, Sidney. *Positive African-American Men-United: A Cultural Revolution.* Nashville, TN: African-American Positive Press, 1994. 118 pp., paperback $19.95. ISBN 1-883-87449-1. This book offers a definition of manhood based on religion, morality and values. The author suggests a concept called the "code of honor" as a template for African-American men to unite and overcome the perils they face in today's society. In addition, he encourages participation of both genders and all races to accomplish this goal.

286. Wood, Peter H. *Black Majority: Negroes in Colonial South Carolina from 1670 through the Stono Rebellion.* New York: W.W. Norton and Co., 1996. 384 pp., paperback $13.95. ISBN 0-393-31482-0. The author blends historical research, anthropological findings, and materials from a variety of scholarly disciplines in his endeavor to reconstruct Black culture in colonial South Carolina. He discusses White reaction to Black culture and discovers a significant number of Africanisms in the Carolina Black population, even the sickle cell anemia trait.

287. Young, R.J. *Antebellum Black Activists: Race, Gender and Self.* New York: Garland Publishers, 1996. 254 pp., includes bibliography and index. ISBN 0-815-31867-7. This book provides insight into antebellum Black activists' sense of self, drawing on original documents from local and state meetings. Also examined is their frequent proclamation, "We are MEN!" in the context of gender, race, and economics of 19th century America. Another focus of the book is how the balancing of public service and private enterprise, one of the few paths to career advancement open to Black men, fostered mutual distrust within the Black community.

11

Leadership

288. Barker, Lucius Jefferson and Walters, Ronald W. (eds.). *Jesse Jackson's 1984 Presidential Campaign: Challenge and Change in American Politics*. Chicago: University of Illinois Press, 1989. 257 pp., includes bibliography and index, hardcover $17.95. ISBN 0-252-06014-8. Jackson was the first Black man who was a serious contender for a majority party nomination. His candidacy for the 1984 Democratic presidential nomination remains one of the most dramatic developments in modern American political history. This book includes the background of the campaign, political expectations, analyses of the Jackson voter, the role of the campaign within the Democratic Party, and the local and national impact of his campaign.

289. Barker, Lucius Jefferson. *Our Time has Come: A Delegate's Diary of Jesse Jackson's 1984 Presidential Campaign*. Urbana: University of Illinois Press, 1988. 223 pp., includes bibliography, hardcover $21.95. ISBN 0-252-01426-X. Discusses Jackson's 1984 presidential campaign. Looks into the achievements of the Black community and the possibility of a Black person being elected to the executive office. Provides an inside view of the primaries.

290. Bositis, David A. *The Congressional Black Caucus in the 103rd Congress*. Washington, DC: University Press of America, 1994. 178 pp., includes bibliography and index, hardcover $57.50, paperback $26.50.

ISBN 0-819-19560-X (H) 0-819-19561-8 (P). A useful reference to the composition of the "new" Congressional Black Caucus with access to reliable and comprehensive information. Includes a critical examination of the individuals within the Caucus and its inner workings. Portrays the importance of the Caucus and the gained appreciation of the group. Expresses the future plans of the organization ranging from lower court rulings to future elections and the changes that will arise with their instigation.

291. Broh, C. Anthony. *A Horse of a Different Color: Television's Treatment of Jesse Jackson's 1984 Presidential Campaign.* Washington, D.C.: Joint Center for Political Studies, 1987. 93 pp., paperback $7.95. ISBN 0-941-41054-4. A political scientist, C. Anthony Broh was commissioned to conduct research on the influence of TV news coverage of Jesse Jackson's 1984 campaign. He analyzed over 2,000 network news programs concerning five of the 1984 Democratic candidates. Broh's research focused on how Jackson's coverage differed from his White competitors' coverage. Specifically, he wanted to know if TV hurt or helped Jackson's chance for success, and ultimately found both were true.

292. Childs, John Brown. *Leadership, Conflict, and Cooperation in Afro-American Social Thought.* Philadelphia: Temple University Press, 1989. 172 pp., includes bibliography, hardcover $27.95, paperback $19.95. ISBN 0-877-22581-8 (H), 1-566-39085-0 (P). Childs writes about Black leadership from 1900 to 1930. He emphasizes two types of leadership: vanguard and mutuality. He characterizes vanguard leaders as those who appreciate the mass but believe they need leadership to direct their goals. He uses Booker T. Washington and W.E.B. DuBois as examples of vanguard leaders. Mutuality leaders placed trust in the people and respected their help in the fight against racism. Leaders George Ellis, Arthur Schomberg and Marcus Garvey were believers in mutuality.

293. Christopher, Maurine. *America's Black Congressmen.* New York: Thomas Y. Crowell Company, 1975. 283 pp., includes bibliography. ISBN 0-815-20376-4. This is a history of African-Americans who served in Congress from 1870 to 1970. Christopher's biographical account of these congressmen includes historical figures such as Senator Hiram R. Revels.

294. Clemente, Frank and Watkins, Frank (eds.). *Keep Hope Alive: Jesse Jackson's 1988 Presidential Campaign.* Boston, MA: South End Press, 1989. 232 pp. ISBN 0-896-08357-8. *Keep Hope Alive* is a collection of major speeches, issue papers, photographs and campaign analysis

regarding Jesse Jackson's 1988 presidential campaign. The book addresses Jackson's campaign message, giving the reader a careful analysis of the core proposals and substance in the Jackson campaign.

295. Collins, Sheila D. *The Rainbow Challenge: The Jackson Campaign and the Future of U.S. Politics.* New York: Monthly Review Press, 1986. 384 pp., hardcover $27.00, paperback $11.00. ISBN 0-853-45691-7. Sheila Collins worked as a field coordinator during the 1984 Jesse Jackson presidential campaign. In this book she describes the development of Jackson's Rainbow Coalition. She also addresses the campaign's endeavor to link top-down bureaucratic organization with bottom-up organization. Collins also analyzes political and social movements that impacted the Jackson campaign and the Rainbow Coalition.

296. Colton, Elizabeth O. *The Jackson Phenomenon: The Man, The Power, The Message.* New York: Doubleday, 1989. 290 pp., hardcover $19.95. ISBN 0-385-26070-9. Colton, former press secretary for the 1988 Jesse Jackson campaign, worked with Jackson for three months. This book is a chronology of the 1987-1988 campaign for the Democratic Party's nomination for President. She focuses on Jackson's progress through the primaries and the Democratic National Convention. Colton also gives an intimate description of Jackson's personality, intellect and ambition.

297. Conti, Joseph G. and Stetson, Brad. *Challenging the Civil Rights Establishment: Profiles of a New Black Vanguard.* Westport, CT: Greenwood Press, 1993. 240 pp., includes bibliography and index, hardcover $22.95. ISBN 0-275-94460-3. This detailed accessible volume analyzes the theories of four prominent Black conservatives--academics Thomas Sowell and Glenn Loury, essayist Shelby Steele, and Robert Woodson, founder of the National Center for Neighborhood Enterprise. The subjects do not see racism as monolithic, are prepared to criticize ghetto culture, and question racially based affirmative action.

298. Davis, Allison. *Leadership, Love, and Aggression.* San Diego, CA: Harcourt Brace Jovanovich, 1983. 260 pp., includes bibliography and index, hardcover $15.95. ISBN 0-151-49348-0. Davis provides a psychological study of the lives of four famous Black American men and leaders. Davis explores the early motivations of Frederick Douglass, W.E.B. DuBois, Richard Wright, and Martin Luther King, Jr. She provides insight into their motivations and philosophies.

299.   Eisinger, Peter K. *The Community Action Program and the Development of Black Political Leadership.* Madison: University of Wisconsin, 1978. 35 pp., includes bibliography. This piece is part of the *Institute for Research in Poverty Discussion Papers* of the University of Wisconsin. Eisinger looks at and assesses the effects of the Community Action Program (CAP) of the Federal War on Poverty on Black political leaders. He studies the effects of CAP on developing Black political leaders and whether it has promoted a different kind of, perhaps more ambitious, leader.

300.   Frady, Marshall. *Jesse: The Life and Pilgrimage of Jesse Jackson.* New York: Random House, 1996. 552 pp., includes bibliography, hardcover $28.50, paperback $16.00. ISBN 0-394-57586-5 (H), 0-679-77845-4 (P). Frady argues that any serious study of Jackson must begin by acknowledging the American crisis of race and recognizing that the gulf between Whites and Blacks remains so deep that there are limits to White writers' understanding. He shows that both are genuine and inextricably linked.

301.   Franklin, John Hope and Meier, August (eds.). *Black Leaders of the Twentieth Century.* Urbana: University of Illinois Press, 1982. 372 pp., includes bibliography and index. ISBN 0-252-00939-8. Two of the leading authorities on Black history in America have joined with other top scholars in the field to create an essential volume on the major achievements of twelve male and three female twentieth century Black leaders. Among the men covered in this book are Booker T. Washington, W.E.B. DuBois, Marcus Garvey, Malcolm X and Martin Luther King, Jr.

302.   Franklin, Robert Michael. *Liberating Visions: Human Fulfillment and Social Justice in African-American Thought.* Minneapolis, MN: Fortress Press, 1990. 174 pp., includes index. ISBN 0-800-62392-4. This book highlights the moral, political, and theological thoughts of Martin Luther King, Jr., Booker T. Washington, W.E.B. DuBois, and Malcolm X. It can help one understand what has shaped the moral development of African-American leaders.

303.   Gaines, Kevin K. *Uplifting the Race: Black Leadership, Politics, and Culture in the Twentieth Century.* Chapel Hill: University of North Carolina Press, 1996. 312 pp., includes bibliography and index, hardcover $45.00, paperback $17.95. ISBN 0-807-82239-6 (H), 0-807-84543-4 (P). In his first three chapters, Gaines outlines some of the problems and concerns of uplift ideology and argues that uplift was not ahead of its times, being neither feminist enough nor sufficiently

concerned with the needs of the lower classes. In the six remaining chapters, he profiles various African-Americans. Gaines helps readers understand the paradox of African-Americans trying to belong to a society defined in part by their exclusion.

304. Gibbons, Arnold. *Race, Politics, and the White Media: The Jesse Jackson Campaigns*. Lanham, MD: University Press of America, 1993. 150 pp., includes bibliography and index, hardcover $44.50, paperback $22.00. ISBN 0-819-18976-6 (H), 0-819-18977-4 (P). Gibbons discusses how the Jackson campaigns brought him closer to the Civil Rights Movement of the 1950s and 1960s.

305. Haskins, Ethelbert W. *The Crisis in Afro-American Leadership*. New York: Prometheus Books, 1988. 196 pp., includes bibliography, hardcover $28.95. ISBN 0-879-75450-8. Haskins examines what he calls the "crisis in Afro-American leadership." He looks at the present problems in Black leadership and suggests possible solutions. He also looks at past leaders such as Frederick Douglas, Booker T. Washington and W.E.B. DuBois as he explores the Black press, education, religion and social morality.

306. Holt, Thomas. *Black over White: Negro Political Leadership in South Carolina During Reconstruction*. Urbana: University of Illinois Press, 1977. 269 pp. ISBN 0-252-00555-6 (H), 0-252-00775-1 (P). Thomas Holt provides an in-depth study of Black leadership in South Carolina during post-Civil War Reconstruction. He attempts to answer many questions regarding Black leadership in South Carolina such as social backgrounds, recruitment and political ideologies. Holt also addresses the reasons for the collapse of Black leadership.

307. Horne, Gerald. *Black Liberation/Red Scare: Ben Davis and the Communist Party*. Newark: University of Delaware Press, 1994. 455 pp., includes bibliography and index, hardcover $55.00. ISBN 0-874-13472-2. Horne focuses on the political life of Benjamin J. Davis, who was a leader among the Communist Party and a major figure in African-American political affairs. Horne depicts the Communist Movement, especially within its Black members, as part of an African-American radical tradition.

308. House, Ernest R. *Jesse Jackson & the Politics of Charisma: The Rise and Fall of the PUSH/Excel Program*. Boulder, CO: Westview Press, Inc., 1988. 196 pp., includes bibliography and index, hardcover $23.95. ISBN 0-813-30767-8. House, a government-funded evaluator of the PUSH/

Excel program, addresses the life and death of the PUSH for excellence program. He suggests that the program failed for four reasons: Jesse Jackson's charismatic style of leadership; the resistance of the public school bureaucracy and the state and local governments to the PUSH/Excel Program; cultural differences between the PUSH/Excel idea and the programmatic expectations of the federal government bureaucracy and its program evaluators; and interethnic conflict between Blacks and Jews.

309. Jackson, Clyde Owen. *Let the Record Show. . . .* Smithtown, NY: Exposition Press, 1983. 95 pp. ISBN 0-682-49985-4. Jackson gives a written account and creates a permanent record of the struggles he and other Black rights activists went through in their quest for civil rights. The book includes letters, news items, editorials, interviews, and speeches that Jackson uses to explain his actions and motivations.

310. Jackson, Jesse, Hatch, Roger D. and Watkins, Frank E. (eds.). *Straight from the Heart.* Philadelphia, PA: Fortress Press, 1987. 324 pp., paperback $18.95. ISBN 0-800-60862-3. This collection of speeches and writings presents Jackson's political vision in the context of his 1988 campaign for the Presidency. It contains thirty-six of his public speeches, sermons, eulogies, essays, and interviews.

311. Kimball, Penn. *Keep Hope Alive!: Super Tuesday and Jesse Jackson's 1988 Campaign for the Presidency.* Washington, D.C.: Joint Center for Political and Economic Studies Press, 1992. 190 pp., hardcover $18.95. ISBN 0-941-41068-4. Kimball analyzes the immediate consequences and the long-range significance of Jesse Jackson's bid for the 1988 Democratic Presidential nomination by profiling his strategy and performance on Super Tuesday.

312. Landess, Thomas H. and Quinn, Richard M. *Jesse Jackson and the Politics of Race.* Ottawa, IL: Jameson Books, First Impressions, Inc., 1985. 269 pp., includes index. ISBN 0-915-46308-3. The authors expose Jesse Jackson's political career and contacts. They detail his career following Martin Luther King, Jr.'s assassination including his famous "Kingdom Theory" speech, programs including PUSH/Excel, his strong association with Louis Farrakhan, and his run for the Presidency in 1984.

313. Lusane, Clarence. *African Americans at the Crossroads: The Restructuring of Black Leadership and the 1992 Elections.* Boston, MA: South End Press, 1994. 262 pp., includes bibliography and index,

hardcover $40.00, paperback $16.00. ISBN 0-896-08468-X (H), 0-896-08469-8 (P). An African-American author, activist, lecturer, and journalist, Lusane analyzes Black politics, and the need for Black political leadership. Lusane, who worked in national Black politics for twenty years, provides a manual for leadership in the African-American community. He highlights race and gender inequality.

314. Marable, Manning. *Black Leadership*. New York: Columbia University Press, 1998. 238 pp., includes bibliography and index, hardcover $31.95. ISBN 0-231-10746-3. At the heart of the book are critical portraits of four Black leaders whose legacies speak to the challenges of race, class, and power: Booker T. Washington, W.E.B. DuBois, Harold Washington, and Louis Farrakhan. The book also identifies three major traditions that have defined American Black political culture: integration, nationalist separatism, and what the author terms democratic transformation.

315. McGriggs, Lee Augustus. *Black Legislative Politics in Illinois: A Theoretical and Structural Analysis.* Lanham, MD: University Press of America, 1977. 200 pp. ISBN 0-819-10336-5. McGriggs analyzes how Blacks in America promote policy that concerns them. He views the Black political experience through statistics. McGriggs identifies the diverse nature of Black politics and finds that if differs from American politics in general. He also locates leadership within the Black community.

316. Miller, Edward A., Jr. *Gullah Statesman: Robert Smalls from Slavery to Congress.* Columbia: University of South Carolina Press, 1995. 285 pp. ISBN 1-570-03002-2. Robert Smalls was a slave who overcame an uneducated past to become a U.S. Congressman from South Carolina. Gullah Statesman traces his roots from sailing on a Confederate supply boat to his prominent career as a Republican Congressman.

317. Morris, Lorenzo (ed.). *The Social and Political Implications of the 1984 Jesse Jackson Presidential Campaign.* New York: Praeger, 1990. 230 pp. ISBN 0-275-92785-7. This book is a collection of essays about the 1984 presidential race and the effects of Jesse Jackson's campaign. Among other things, Morris addresses the impact of Jackson's campaign on Black prospects and how his proposals related to the Black public. He concludes that Jesse Jackson is a very influential political leader.

318. Morrison, Minion K.C. *Black Political Mobilization: Leadership, Power and Mass Behavior.* Albany: State University of New York Press, 1987. 303 pp., hardcover $44.50, paperback $19.95. ISBN 0-887-06515-5 (H),

0-887-06516-3 (P). In this text, Minion Morrison analyzes the improvement in Black electoral participation in the years following passage of the Voting Rights Act of 1965. He focuses on three small Mississippi towns in this study: Bolton, Mayersville, and Tchula.

319. Nelson, Albert J. *Emerging Influentials in State Legislatures: Women, Blacks and Hispanics.* New York: Praeger, 1991. 136 pp. ISBN 0-275-93829-8. This book attempts to summarize the role of minority groups in State politics. Nelson addresses where and how much influence women, Blacks and Hispanics hold. He also looks at the impact representatives have on these groups. Nelson gives statistical data to explore the issues of turnover and influence.

320. Nordin, Dennis S. *The New Deal's Black Congressman: A Life of Arthur Wergs Mitchell.* Columbia: University of Missouri Press, 1997. 320 pp., hardcover $55.50. ISBN 0-826-21102-X. Nordin's book is a "biographical sketch" of Arthur Wergs Mitchell, the first Black Democrat elected to Congress. He examines how Mitchell worked within the system and to gain a foothold of power before taking on a more civil rights-oriented agenda. Nordin argues that Mitchell is in large measure responsible for bringing Blacks into leadership positions within the Democratic Party.

321. Perry, Robert T. *Black Legislators.* San Francisco: R and E Research Associates, 1976. 165 pp., includes bibliography. IBSN 0-882-47389-1. This book is an analysis of the 13 Black members of the Missouri House of Representatives during the 1969-1970 session. Missouri had more Black members than any other state at the time. Perry compares these legislators with their White colleagues and finds that they came from more economically deprived backgrounds, were more likely to be born outside the U.S., were a little older, and were more apt to be involved in the Civil Rights Movement and the NAACP. Perry also examines their voting patterns.

322. Pitre, Merline. *Through Many Dangers, Toils, and Snares: The Black Leadership of Texas, 1868-1900.* Austin, TX: Eakin Press, 1985. 260 pp., $15.95. ISBN 0-890-15524-0. This study examines the nature of Black political leadership in Texas in the late nineteenth century. A biographical section provides a look at the careers of five prominent leaders--Matthew Gaines, George T. Ruby, Richard Allen, Robert L. Smith, and Norris Wright Cuney. Pitre argues that the influence of Black leaders was ultimately limited by White racism and that White opposition was the major force restricting Black office holding.

323. Rabinowitz, Howard N. (ed.). *Southern Black Leaders of the Reconstruction Era*. Urbana, IL: University of Illinois Press, 1982. 422 pp., includes bibliography and index, hardcover $27.50, paperback $9.95. ISBN 0-252-00972-X (P). Rabinowitz provides basic biographical information, determines positions on major issues, and reveals how Blacks functioned within Reconstruction and Republican politics.

324. Ragsdale, Bruce A. and Treese, Joel D. *Black Americans in Congress: 1870-1989*. Washington, DC: U.S. G.P.O., 1990. 164 pp., includes bibliography, paperback $15.00. ISBN 0-160-18476-2. This volume presents biographies of all Black Americans who have served in Congress. Each entry features a photograph or illustration of the legislator and an approximately one-page biography, focusing on the individual's accomplishments as a member of Congress.

325. Reed, Cecil A. with Donovan, Priscilla. *Fly in the Buttermilk: The Life Story of Cecil Reed*. Iowa City: University of Iowa Press, 1993. 184 pp., hardcover $29.95, paperback $13.95. ISBN 0-877-45415-9 (H), 0-877-45416-7 (P). This book chronicles the life of Cecil Reed, who grew up an isolated Midwestern African-American in the early 20th century. He managed to succeed in the White world, ultimately getting elected to state and federal offices with substantial responsibility over various job programs. Reed embraced the system to gain entrance into politics.

326. Reynolds, Barbara A. *Jesse Jackson: The Man, The Movement, The Myth*. New York: Nelson-Hall, 1975. 489 pp., includes index, $9.95. ISBN 0-911012-80-X. Reynolds' biography of Jackson is set in the struggle for national Black leadership after the assassination of Martin Luther King, Jr. She writes in a journalistic style and bases her book on first-hand observations of Jackson. She explores his theories and personality as she looks at leadership problems in the Black community. Reynolds offers suggestions for changes in future leadership developments.

327. Richardson, James. *Willie Brown: A Biography*. Berkeley, CA: University of California Press, 1996. 509 pp., includes bibliography and index, hardcover $29.95, paperback $17.95. ISBN 0-520-20456-5 (H), 0-520-21315-7 (P). In this profile of San Francisco's mayor, Richardson details Brown's rise to power and remarkable achievements, showing how he built a power base and how his strategizing has kept progressive politics alive in California.

328. Smith, Robert C. *Black Leadership: A Survey of Theory and Research.* Washington, DC: Mental Health Research and Development Center, Institute for Urban Affairs and Research, Howard University. This study, divided into the old Negro leadership literature (1930-1966) and the new Black leadership literature (1966-1982), is organized around four major categories of analysis. These include the structure of power in the Black community, the social background characteristics of Black leaders, Black political organizations and Black leadership ideologies and strategies. Factors affecting the transformation in the 1960s from Negro to Black leadership are specified and analyzed. A concluding chapter presents the tasks and responsibilities of Black leadership in the continuing struggle for racial justice.

329. Swain, Carol M. *Black Faces, Black Interests: The Representation of African Americans in Congress.* Cambridge, MA: Harvard University Press, 1993. 275 pages, includes index and bibliographic references, hardcover $42.50, paperback $16.50. ISBN 0-674-07615 (H), 0-674-07616-8 (P). Swain investigates the representation of Blacks in politics. This book reveals how and who is representing the Black population as it brings to light the question of fair and just representation. Swain addresses the question of whether Blacks are being fairly and justly represented in the political arena.

330. Vincent, Charles. *Black Legislators in Louisiana during Reconstruction.* Baton Rouge: Louisiana State University Press, 1976. 262 pp., includes bibliography, hardcover $15.00. ISBN 0-807-10089-7. Vincent confronts the myth of illiterate Black legislators dominating state politics from the end of the Civil War until 1877. Rather than illiterate ex-slaves, Vincent finds literate individuals, often experienced in business or public life, who were well qualified to hold office. He argues that these legislators performed their duties with integrity, intelligence, and compassion.

331. White, John. *Black Leadership in America: From Booker T. Washington to Jesse Jackson.* New York: Longman, Inc., 1990. 223 pp., paperback $17.95. ISBN 0-582-06372-8. White begins this volume with an overview of early Black protest and leadership focusing on such individuals as Gabriel Prosser, Denmark Vesey, Nat Turner, and especially Frederick Douglass. Convinced that African-American history is basically "a history of the conflict between integrationist and nationalist forces in politics, economics and culture" (p.1), White argues that Blacks have had only limited opportunities to select their own leaders. He finds

that Black leaders have historically been dependent on White as well as Black recognition of their claims as racial spokesmen.

332. Williams, Lea Esther. *Servants of the People: The 1960s Legacy of African American Leadership*. New York: St. Martin's Press, 1996. 251 pp., includes bibliography and index, hardcover $39.95, paperback $15.95. ISBN 0-312-16372-X (H), 0-312-17684-8 (P). The book begins with an overview of African-American history from reconstruction to the civil rights era. Williams profiles African-Americans who rose to prominence during the civil rights movement. These leaders headed Black churches, Black colleges, and civil rights and social service organizations. Williams devotes a chapter to each leader, and concludes by addressing contemporary leadership issues and the legacy of the Civil Rights Movement.

333. Woody, Bette. *Managing Crisis Cities: The New Black Leadership and the Politics of Resource Allocation*. Westport, CT: Greenwood Press, 1982. 228 pp., $27.50. ISBN 0-313-23095-1. In this study, Woody surveys various urban policies and reforms during the 1970s and early 1980s in an effort to explain their failure in resolving the urban economic crisis. She analyzes five cities (LA, New Orleans, Oakland, Detroit, and Newark) under the administration of Black mayors and examines their reform strategies and constraints that have hindered reformism.

12

Media and Literature

334. Aptheker, Herbert. *The Literary Legacy of W.E.B. DuBois*. White Plains, NY: Kraus International Publications, 1989. 371 pp., includes bibliography and index, paperback $14.95. ISBN 0-527-03693-5. Aptheker, a professor, former Guggenheim Fellow and personal friend of DuBois, has compiled a complete and revised edition of DuBois's introductory essays from the Kraus editions (which are book-length works of DuBois). These introductory essays provide an overview of DuBois' literary life and contributions.

335. Boskin, Joseph. *Sambo: The Rise and Demise of an American Jester*. New York: Oxford University Press, 1986. 252 pp., includes bibliography and index, hardcover $23.95. IBSN 0-195-05658-2. This book talks about the stereotyped character of Sambo and how he entertained White Americans and Europeans as a vehicle of racial humor. Boskin draws on many sources to trace the evolution of Sambo, and how he died during the Civil Rights Movement in the 1960s. This study provides insight into American race relations in this period.

336. Dudley, David L. *My Father's Shadow: Intergenerational Conflict in African American Men's Autobiography*. Philadelphia: University of Pennsylvania Press, 1991. 218 pp., includes bibliography and index, hardcover $24.95. ISBN 0-812-23081-7. Dudley examines Black men's autobiography focusing on authors such as Frederick Douglass, Booker T.

Washington, and W.E.B. DuBois. He finds similarities in their works, but also identifies their individual nature.

337. Fredrickson, George M. *The Black Image in the White Mind: The Debate on Afro-American Character and Destiny, 1817-1914.* New York: Wesleyan University Press, 1991. 347 pp., includes bibliography and index, paperback $19.95. ISBN 0-8195-6188-6. Fredrickson attempts to explain the "development of intellectualized racist theory and ideology." He discusses the ways in which Whites think about Blacks. He examines the impact of pseudoscientific racism on racial attitudes and provides a history of racial ideas.

338. Hutchinson, Earl Ofari. *The Assassination of the Black Male Image.* Simon & Schuster, 1996. 208 pp., $20.00. ISBN 0-684-83100-7. Hutchinson writes that the "myth of the malevolent Black male is based on a durable and time-resistant bedrock of myths, half-truths and lies." He criticizes media portrayals of Black men, derisive words used to describe Black athletes and the media attention given to *Waiting to Exhale*'s portrayal of Black men. Hutchinson argues violence and poverty in society cause Black violence.

339. Leab, Daniel J. *From Sambo to Superspade: The Black Experience in Motion Pictures.* Boston: Houghton Mifflin, 1976. 301 pp., includes bibliography, hardcover $19.00. IBSN 0-395-19402-4. Leab uses sources from both Black and White filmmakers to demonstrate the negative portrayal of Blacks in movies. He analyzes stereotypes and investigates the evolution of the Black image in motion pictures.

340. Richburg, Keith B. *Out of Africa: A Black Man Confronts Africa.* San Diego, CA: Harcourt Brace & Company, 1998. 266 pp., includes index, paperback $13.00. ISBN 0-15-600583-2. Confessing what may be a cardinal sin in multiculturalist America, Mr. Richburg concludes that, having lived in Africa for three years and seen what he describes as its horrors, he can no longer bring himself to proudly claim an African-American identity. Instead, he is quite simply, and gratefully an American--a Black American. Richburg is an international journalist who has provided an honest, compelling and insightful account of his personal experiences in Africa.

341. Turner, Patricia A. *Ceramic Uncles and Celluloid Mammies: Black Images and Their Influence on Culture.* New York: Anchor Books, 1994. 238 pp., includes bibliography, index, and illustrations, paperback $12.95. ISBN 0-385-46784-2. This book is a study of Black representation in

American popular culture. Turner documents how cultural artifacts from 150 years ago to the present reinforce long-standing stereotypes of African-Americans. She explores other issues, including the legacy of 19th century minstrelsy and Harriet Beecher Stowe's *Uncle Tom's Cabin*, and the film industry's portrayal of African-Americans.

13

Religion

342. Burke, Ronald K. *Samuel Ringgold Ward: Christian Abolitionist.* New York: Garland Publishing Co., 1995. 165 pp., includes bibliography and index, hardcover $42.00. ISBN 0-815-31930-4. A Maryland fugitive slave, Ward was a leader in the abolitionist movement. Burke describes his experiences in the 1840s and 1850s as a minister to White churches in upstate New York. He also addresses his work with fugitive slaves in Canada, and his eventual relocation to Jamaica after being accused of fraud in 1855.

343. Burkett, Randall K. and Newman, Richard (eds.). *Black Apostles: Afro-American Clergy Confront the Twentieth Century.* Boston: G.K. Hall, 1978. ISBN 0-816-18137-3. The authors discuss African intellectual influences on Black Americans. They analyze Edward W. Blyden's role in this process. The book contains notes on Arnold J. Ford and New World Black attitudes towards Ethiopia. Also included are topics concerning racism, World War I, and the Christian life.

344. Childs, John Brown. *The Political Black Minister: A Study in Afro-American Politics and Religion.* Boston, MA: G.K. Hall, 1980. 153 pp., includes bibliography and index, $18.50. ISBN 0-816-19023-2. Childs provides a case study of three Black ministers from Buffalo, NY who were politically active. He explores their political and religious reactions to problems in the Black community.

345. Corrothers, James D. *In Spite of the Handicap: An Autobiography.* Westport, CT: Negro Universities Press, 1977. 238 pp., $69.00. ISBN 0-836-98884-1. This book was considered one of the best autobiographies of the 1970s. It came at a time when Blacks were still looked down upon, and it exemplified the pain and suffering they were going through.

346. Foley, A.S. *God's Men of Color: The Colored Catholic Priests of the U.S., 1854-1954.* New York: Arno Press, 1969. 338 pp., paperback $23.95. ISBN 0-405-01864-9. These are biographical accounts of Black parish priests, army chaplains, and college and seminary teachers. Each chapter relates their achievements and the obstacles they faced.

347. Franklin, Rev. C.L., Todd, Jeff (ed.), Jackson, Jesse (designer). *Give Me this Mountain: Life History and Selected Sermons.* Champaign: University of Illinois Press, 1989. 240 pp., paperback $14.95. ISBN 0-252-06087-3. Designed by Jesse Jackson, this text contains numerous stories and sermons from one of the most credited Black religious leaders of our time. C.L. Franklin was considered a prophet and is still widely imitated in preaching style.

348. June, Lee N. and Parker, Matthew (eds.). *Men to Men: Perspectives of Fifteen African-American Christian Men.* Grand Rapids, MI: Zondervan Publishing House, 1996. 240 pp., paperback $12.99. ISBN 0-310-20157-8. This is a powerful collection of essays by Black male Christian scholars written to Black men on issues that concern them today. Selected titles include, Risk and Failure as Preludes to Achievements, The Criminal Justice System: A Message to Young Black Males, and more.

349. Kunjufu, Jawanza. *Adam! Where are You?: Why Most Black Men Don't Go to Church.* Chicago, IL: African American Images, 1997. 148 pp., paperback $10.95. ISBN 0-91354-343-8. Kunjufu offers insight into why most Black males no longer attend church. He asks questions about why women dominate the church by a 75 percent margin and also why the Black male's presence is stronger in the Islamic faith than in the Christian faith. He also addresses the question of how the Black man can restore his faith in God.

350. Lawrence, Beverly Hall. *Reviving the Spirit: A Generation of African-Americans Goes Home to Church.* New York: Grove Press, 1996. Paperback $11.00. ISBN 0-80213-499-8. Sister Lawrence writes about the spiritual lives of middle-class African-Americans through her own experiences and interviews with members of the Bethel African Methodist Episcopal Church in Baltimore. She discusses why Black people are

returning to church in very high numbers and examines exactly what the church means to the Black community. Lawrence predicts a social change through this resurgence of faith.

351. Paris, Peter J. *Black Religious Leaders: Conflict in Unity*. Louisville, KY: Westminster/John Knox Press, 1991. 326 pp., includes bibliography, paperback $20.00. ISBN 0-664-25145-5. This scholarly book offers a distinctive analysis of four Black religious leaders: Joseph H. Jackson, Martin Luther King, Jr., Adam Clayton Powell, Jr., and Malcolm X. Paris classifies the four as priestly, prophetic, political, and nationalist.

352. Robinson, James H. *Road without Turning: The Story of Reverend James H. Robinson*. New York: Farrar, Straus, 1950. 312 pp. ISBN 0-02687-844-7. A self portrayal that instead of looking only at the great times in his life looks at him as a middle aged man that was still trying to conquer the weaknesses that all in the human race have. An honest look at his beliefs, doubts, hatred, despair and self-pity.

353. Rooks, Charles Shelby. *Revolution in Zion: Reshaping African American Ministry, 1960-1974: A Biography in the First Person*. New York: Pilgrim Press, 1990. 234 pp. ISBN 0-8298-0873-6. This text reflects Rooks' mission to get more Black people into the Christian ministry. He tells stories of victory and defeat about what his revolution had to go through. His story is set against the Civil Rights Struggle of the 1960s and 1970s.

354. Sharpton, Al with Walton, Anthony. *Go and Tell Pharaoh: The Autobiography of Reverend Al Sharpton*. New York: Doubleday, 1996. 276 pp., includes index, hardcover $23.95. ISBN 0-385-47583-7. Reverend Al Sharpton's autobiography addresses how Blacks like Martin Luther King, Jr., James Brown, and Don King have influenced his person, which is known to be a race agitator. He recounts his involvement with the FBI and racial incidences like those in Howard Beach, Crown Heights, and Bensonhurst.

355. Swift, David E. *Black Prophets of Justice: Activist Clergy Before the Civil War*. Baton Rouge: Louisiana State University Press, 1989. 384 pp. ISBN 0-80711-461-8. Swift's book tells the history of protest against racism. His study includes religious figures Samuel Cornish, Theodore Wright, Charles Ray, Henry Highland Garnet, Amos Beman, and James W.C. Pennington.

356. Thomas, Herman E. *James W.C. Pennington: African-American Churchman and Abolitionist*. New York: Garland Publishers, 1995. 206 pp., includes bibliography, hardcover $51.00. ISBN 0-815-31889-8. Thomas writes about the life and struggles of James Pennington, a fugitive blacksmith who became a clergyman and a leading abolitionist. His main argument is that Pennington exhibited the dual functions of African-American religion with his focus on "other-worldliness" and his "this-worldly" commitment to abolitionist activities. Thomas also discusses Pennington's opposition to African colonization efforts and his support of missionaries in Africa.

357. Walker, Beersheba C. *Life and Works of William Saunders Crowdy*. Philadelphia, PA: E.J.P. Walker, 1995. 62 pp. This biography of Crowdy was compiled with the help of Bishop Joseph Brent, Evg. James Delany, Elder Rufus Mundy, and Crowdy himself. This book documents the journey of a young African-American from his birth in Maryland through the turbulent times of the mid- to late-19th century. The journey eventually leads him to create the Church of God and Saints of Christ.

358. Watts, Jill. *God, Harlem, USA: The Father Divine Story*. Berkeley: University of California Press, 1992. 249 pp., includes bibliography and index, hardcover $40.00, paperback $14.95. ISBN 0-520-07455-6 (H), 0-520-20172-8 (P). Born George Baker, Jr. (1876-1965), Father Divine was a charismatic African-American religious leader. In this expansion of Watt's doctoral thesis, the author argues that Father Divine should be recognized as a theologian rather than a cult figure. This meticulously researched book provides a detailed portrait of an influential African-American.

359. Wheeler, Edward L. *Uplifting the Race: The Black Minister in the New South, 1865-1902*. Lanham, MD: University Press of America, 1986. 146 pp., includes bibliography, paperback $11.75. ISBN 0-8191-5162-9 (H), 0-8191-5161-0 (P). Wheeler examines the writings and careers of seventy-eight Southern Black ministers of the late nineteenth century. He uses 'uplift' to describe the goals of Black ministerial leaders. Wheeler provides a solid contribution to our understanding of the role of the Black church during post-Civil War years.

360. White, George. *Brief Account of the Life, Experience, Travels, and Gospel Labours of George White, an African*. Madison, WI: Madison House, 1993. 200 pp., includes index, hardcover $26.95. ISBN 0-945612-32-X. White, founder of the African Methodist Episcopal Zion denomination, offers valuable insight and a rare glimpse into the

liberating theology of Freed Northern slaves. He explores their adjustment to their new position in Northern society and Methodist Christianity and tells of his own conflicts with White Methodist officials.

361. Williams, Ethel L. *Biographical Directory of Negro Ministers*. Metuchen, NJ: Scarecrow Press, Inc., 1975.   605 pp., includes bibliography. ISBN 0-816-11183-9. This is an extensive compilation of biographies of Black ministers from around the country and from all denominations with pertinent contact information.

362. Wills, David W. and Newman, Richard. *Black Apostles: At Home and Abroad*. Boston, MA: G.K. Hall & Co., 1982. 321 pp., includes index. ISBN 0-8161-8482-8. Wills and Newman provide a collective portrait of some of the leading figures in Black religious life in the period between the Revolution and Reconstruction. They attempt to provide a wide representation of Black religious life during this period.

363. Wright, Richard R., Jr. *87 Years Behind the Black Curtain: An Autobiography*. Philadelphia, PA: Rare Book Co., 1965. 351 pp., includes index. (Out of print--no ISBN available.) Wright provides an extensive background on his life as a Black man through an elaborate research of old letters, public records, newspapers, and other sources. He tells of his consciousness of his experiences in the American Christian climate ranging from his home to the world as a whole. Wright provides an historical perspective of the life of a first-generation educated free Black man.

14

Sports

364. Ashe, Arthur. *Arthur Ashe: Portrait in Motion.* Carroll and Graf Publishers, 1993. 272 pp., paperback $11.95. ISBN 0-786-70050-5. This book takes a unique approach. It is a day-to-day diary that Ashe kept for a year from Wimbledon in 1973 to Wimbledon in 1974. It details his sensitivity to his role as a ground-breaker in the world of tennis because of his race. The book provides a personal portrait of Ashe because these are his thoughts, his ideas, and his feelings. It lists his flights, hotels and other everyday events.

365. Ashe, Arthur with Amdur, Neil. *Arthur Ashe: Off the Court.* New York: New American Library Books, 1981. 219 pp., $13.95. ISBN 0-453-00400-8. In this book, tennis star Ashe talks freely and frankly about all that has happened to him, and all he has done and felt. He talks about growing up in the segregated South in the 1950s and 1960s. He traces his collegiate and professional career, as well as his family, and his competitors. It includes photographs and a chronology of his tennis career.

366. Ashe, Arthur with Branch, Kip, Chalk, Ocania, and Harris, Francis. *A Hard Road to Glory: A History of the African-American Athlete.* New York: Warner Books, 1988. Includes bibliography and index. Volume 1: 1619-1918, 194 pp., $29.95, ISBN 0-446-71008-3. Volume 2: 1919-1945, 497 pp., $39.95, ISBN 0-446-71007-5. Volume 3: From 1946, 571

pp., $39.95, ISBN 0-446-71008-3. The former tennis champion and his collaborators compile a three-volume historical record of African-American athletic accomplishments for the past 300+ years. Along with their accomplishments, the authors document the prejudices and barriers Blacks have had to overcome in their respective spots. They list every sport Blacks have played and include a reference section of records divided by sport.

367. Ashe, Arthur and Rampersad, Arnold. *Days of Grace: A Memoir*. New York: Alfred A. Knopf, 1993. 317 pp., includes index, hardcover $24.00, paperback $6.99.   ISBN 0-679-42396-6 (H), 0-345-38681-7 (P, Ballantine Books). This is a memoir by Ashe that embodies his courage and grace in every aspect of his life, from his triumphs as a great tennis champion and his determined social activism to his ordeal with AIDS. He discusses issues such as his life as an athlete, sexual promiscuity in the world of professional sports, and the controversy of educational standards for college athletics.

368. Astor, Gerald. *". . . And a Credit to His Race": The Hard Life and Times of Joseph Louis Barrow, a.k.a. Joe Louis*. New York: Saturday Review Press, 1974. 275 pp., $7.95. ISBN 0-841-50347-8. Astor chronicles the events surrounding Joe Louis' championship fight. He also details the hard times of his life in an attempt to help the reader understand some of Louis' decisions.   Astor gives an account of Louis' participation in sometimes questionable behaviors. He argues that Louis was unaware of the significance his fight had on the Black community.

369. Baker, William J. *Jesse Owens: An American Life*. New York: The Free Press, 1986. 289 pp., includes bibliography and index, hardcover $19.95, paperback $14.95. ISBN 0-029-01780-7 (H), 0-029-01760-2 (P). This book chronicles Owens' life story from his birth in Jim Crow Alabama to his exploits in Berlin's Olympic Stadium, to his final battle with lung cancer. Baker shows how Owens' personality, achievements, and image fulfilled a cultural need beyond the athletic arena.

370. Bankes, James. *The Pittsburgh Crawfords: The Lives & Times of Black Baseball's Most Exciting Team*. Dubuque, IA: Wm. C. Brown, 1991. 173 pp., includes index and illustrations, $15.95. ISBN 0-697-12889-X. Bankes shares the history of the Pittsburgh Crawfords, a Black baseball team. He looks at baseball great Satchel Paige and his role in paving the way for Jackie Robinson. Bankes tells how Black baseball teams proved their worth. He recounts incidents of the players' lives away from the

baseball diamond and how well they represented their race on and off the playing field.

371. Bell, Marty. *The Legend of Dr. J.* New York: Coward McCann and Geoghegan, Inc., 1975. 208 pp. ISBN 0-698-10639-3. Bell gives a detailed account of the fame and fortune of basketball legend Dr. J. Julius Erving, unlike many other basketball greats, appeared on the basketball scene as his college days were ending. He became one of the greatest men ever to play the game and was regarded as a great player on and off the court.

372. Brooks, Dana and Althouse, Ronald. *Racism in College Athletics.* Morgantown, WV: Fitness Information Technology, Inc., 1993. 303 pp., includes bibliography and index, hardcover $38.00. ISBN 0-962-79262-4. Brooks and Althouse argue that racism pervades sports and they offer solutions to this problem. They cover the entire history of Blacks in sports as well as the history of athletic racism. They offer strategies for athletes to combat racism.

373. Bruce, Janet. *The Kansas City Monarchs: Champions of Black Baseball.* Lawrence, KS: University Press of Kansas, 1991. 176 pp., includes bibliography and index, paperback $12.95. ISBN 0-700-60273-9 (H), 0-700-60343-3 (P). This study analyzes the significance of the Kansas City Monarchs as a Black urban social institution. It includes photographs and personal stories that highlight the top Black baseball team.

374. Chalk, Ocania. *Pioneers in Black Sport: The Early Days of the Black Professional Athlete in Baseball, Basketball, Boxing, and Football.* New York: Dodd, Mead, and Company, 1975. 305 pp., includes bibliography and index, $7.95. ISBN 0-396-06868-5. This book tells the story of Black athletes who broke down the barriers that prevented them from emerging with White athletes in professional baseball, basketball, boxing, and football. Chalk attempts to "set the record straight" for those names that have been obscured by White dominance in sports.

375. Clark, Dick and Lester, Larry (eds.). *The Negro Leagues Book.* Cleveland, Ohio: Society for American Baseball Research 1994. 382 pp., includes bibliography, hardcover $49.95, paperback $29.95. ISBN 0-910-13759-5 (H), 0-910-13755-2 (P). Based on the work of the Negro Leagues Committee of the Society of American Baseball Research, this book provides a history of Black baseball. It also includes biographies of Negro Leaguers, team names, the cities they represented, and records held by Negro League players.

376. Davis, Lenwood G. *Joe Louis: A Bibliography of Articles, Books, Pamphlets, Records, and Archival Materials.* Westport, CT: Greenwood Press, 1983. 232 pp., $29.99. ISBN 0-313-23327-6. Heavyweight champion Joe Louis was a symbol of Black excellence and pride in the 1930s and 1940s. This comprehensive reference book provides a brief biographical sketch and close to 2800 entries. The bibliography is divided into sections that cover his life in boxing, family life, business, and Army experiences. Each section is arranged chronologically and covers the period from 1934 to 1982.

377. Davis, Lenwood G. and Daniels, Belinda S. *Black Athletes in the United States: A Bibliography of Books, Articles, Autobiographies, and Biographies on Black Professional Athletes in the United States, 1800-1981.* Westport, CT: Greenwood Press, 1981. 265 pp., includes index, hardcover $29.95. ISBN 0-313-22976-7. This bibliography covers baseball, basketball, boxing, football, golf, and tennis. It includes a variety of sources including vertical files, scrapbooks, letters, and doctoral dissertations. It has lists of Most Valuable Players from baseball and basketball, a chronological list of Black boxing champions, and the names of Hall of Fame members.

378. Dixon, Phil with Hannigan, Patrick J. *The Negro Baseball Leagues: A Photographic History.* Mattituck, NY: Amereon House, 1992. 329 pp., includes bibliography and index. ISBN 0-848-80425-2. This collection of over 600 photographs chronicles the most familiar and unfamiliar names in Negro baseball. This is a complete picture of the Negro Leagues and the people who were part of it. The text challenges myths surrounding the Leagues.

379. Dorsett, Tony and Frommer, Harvey. *Running Tough: Memoirs of a Football Maverick.* New York: Doubleday, 1989. 225 pp., hardcover $17.95. ISBN 0-385-26248-5. In this book, Dorsett offers a detailed inside look at the NFL, its players, and the Dallas Cowboys in particular. Along with personal history, he addresses drug use among players, media stereotyping, the excesses of college recruiting, and his controversial trade to the Denver Broncos. This autobiography includes his reactions and adjustments to newfound prejudices in Texas, and his relationships with players and coaches.

380. Farr, Finis. *Black Champion: The Life and Times of Jack Johnson.* New York: Scribner, 1964. 237 pp. Jack Johnson was the first Black heavyweight boxing champion. Born 15 years after the end of the Civil War, Johnson became rich and famous because of his amazing physical

strength and stamina. In this biography, Farr chronicles the career and personal life of this controversial champion and concludes that he was a giant figure who paved the way for African-Americans to gain major sport stardom.

381. Garrity, John (ed.). *Tiger Woods: The Making of a Champion.* New York: Simon and Schuster, 1996. 94 pp., hardcover $20.00, paperback $10.95. ISBN 0-684-84226-2 (H), 0-684-84462-1 (P). Excerpted from *Sports Illustrated*, the writers trace Tiger's rise to the top of the golfing world. Complete with photographs and SI's great commentary this is a thorough chronicle of Tiger's career.

382. George, Nelson. *Elevating the Game: Black Men and Basketball.* New York: HarperCollins Publisher, Inc., 1992. 261 pp., includes bibliography and index, hardcover $20.00. ISBN 0-060-16723-8. George examines the role of Black men in basketball, and how basketball has provided a public arena for Black men to earn respect as they display their grace and athletic ability.

383. Greene, Bob. *Rebound: The Odyssey of Michael Jordan.* New York: Viking Press, 1995. 275 pp., paperback $5.99. ISBN 0-451-19157-9. Michael Jordan is a national icon and one of the country's most well-known and fascinating basketball players. In touching detail, Jordan discusses with Bob Greene his personal journey and experiences in basketball.

384. Haskins, James. *Doctor J.: A Biography of Julius Erving.* Garden City, NY: Doubleday, 1975. 94 pp. ISBN 0-385-09906-1 (H), 0-385-09905-3 (P). As a 5'9" guard, Julius Erving of the New York Nets was one of the most colorful ballplayers of all times. Haskins offers an adequate look at this excellent player who is also a fine human being.

385. Holway, John B. *Black Diamonds: Life in the Negro Leagues from the Men Who Lived It.* Westport, CT: Meckler Books, 1989. 189 pp., includes index, hardcover $32.50. ISBN 0-887-36334-2. This book brings back to life, in their own words, the times, characters, and playing careers of eleven men who starred in the Negro Leagues.

386. Holway, John B. *Voices from the Great Black Baseball Leagues.* New York: Da Capo Press, 1992. 363 pp., includes index, paperback $14.95. ISBN 0-848-81566-1 (H), 0-306-80470-0 (P). Holway has gathered five decades of Black baseball history, compiled from interviews with more than 70 former players. Along with a history of Black baseball he

examines the achievements of well-known players such as Jackie
Robinson and Satchel Paige.

387. Jakoubek, Robert E. *Jack Johnson*. New York: Chelsea House, 1990.
     111 pp., includes bibliography and index, paperback $19.95. ISBN 0-
     791-01113-5. Describes the life of the Black man who won the
     heavyweight championship boxing title in 1908. Jakoubek provides a
     detailed account of the achievements, personality, and personal life of
     Jack Johnson.

388. Johnson, Earvin "Magic." *Magic's Touch*. Reading, MA: Addison
     Wesley Longman, Inc., 1989. 236 pp., includes illustrations, $17.95.
     ISBN 0-685-26629-X (H), 0-201-51794-9 (P). This book is filled with
     great stories about Magic's father, teammates, coaches, and rivals. It
     provides a message from Magic about team effort based on respect and
     communication.

389. Johnson, Earvin "Magic" with Novak, William. *My Life*. New York:
     Random House, 1992. 332 pp., includes illustrations, hardcover $22.00,
     paperback $5.99. ISBN 0-679-41569-6 (H), 0-449-22254-3 (P). In this
     autobiography, Johnson writes of his life--his family and friends, his
     basketball career, and his brave fight against the virus that causes AIDS.

390. Jordan, Michael. *Rare Air: Michael on Michael*. San Francisco, CA:
     HarperCollins Publishers, 1993. 111 pp. ISBN 0-00-255389-9 (H), 0-00-
     638256-8 (P). Jordan discusses competition and the Blackness that
     embodies him. He discusses how the U.S. sees him as representative of
     all Black athletes.

391. Krugel, Mitchell. *Jordan: The Man, His Words, His Life*. New York: St.
     Martin's Press, 1994. 277 pp., hardcover $21.95, paperback $5.99. ISBN
     0-312-11090-1 (H), 0-312-95814-5 (P). This book, written by a Chicago
     sportswriter and friend of Jordan's, features interviews and conversations
     in Jordan's own words. He covers his entrance into the NBA in 1984
     through the 1993 season. Krugel relates stories about Jordan's most
     memorable moments in the game and how he handles the spotlight. Top
     players and coaches in the league also share what it is like to coach and
     play with and against Jordan.

392. Louis, Joe. *Joe Louis: My Life*. New York: Ecco Press, 1997. 277 pp.,
     paperback $11.00. ISBN 0-880-01532-2. African-American
     heavyweight boxing champion Joe Louis tells the story of his life. Louis
     begins with growing up in poverty without a father and continues through

his entrance into and battle to the top of boxing. He provides vivid details of his triumphs as a boxer and his problems with drugs, taxes, and women.

393. Mailor, Norman. *The Fight*. Boston: Little, Brown and Company, 1975. 239 pp., hardcover $7.95. ISBN 0-316-54416-7. Mailor writes of what happened in the ring between two great heavy-weight boxers: Muhammad Ali and George Foreman. He gives a close-up look at each fighter, trainer, and the media.

394. McPhee, John. *Levels of the Game*. New York: Farrar, Straus & Giroux, 1979. Paperback $9.00. ISBN 0-374-51526-3. McPhee details Arthur Ashe's life and achievements. He follows Ashe throughout his journey to the top of tennis. This book depicts the life and controversy faced by this great athlete.

395. Mead, Chris. *Champion--Joe Louis: Black Hero in White America*. New York: Charles Scribner's Sons, 1995. 330 pp., includes bibliography and index, $18.95. ISBN 0-860-51848-5. This portrait of Joe Louis shows his rise through virulent racism to his emergence as a major public figure and athlete. Mead recreates Louis' major fights from ringside films.

396. Moore, Joseph Thomas. *Pride Against Prejudice: The Biography of Larry Doby*. Westport, CT: Greenwood Press, 1988. 195 pp., includes bibliography, index and illustrations, hardcover $49.95, paperback $14.95. ISBN 0-313-25995-X (H), 0-275-92984-1 (P). This book shows that Larry Doby, a Black baseball player, was a civil rights pioneer. Moore examines his role in integrating baseball and his impact as a player. The author argues that Doby was seen as a typical player to whom the average Black man could relate.

397. Naughton, Jim. *Taking to the Air: The Rise of Michael Jordan*. New York: Warner Books, 1992. 264 pp., includes index, hardback $18.95. ISBN 0-446-51629-5 (H), 0-446-36401-0 (P). Naughton provides a behind the scenes biography of Jordan. He gives a detailed description of his basketball career and the role his parents, teammates, and family have played in his life. He also describes Jordan's involvement with Nike and other business ventures.

398. Peterson, Robert. *Only the Ball was White: A History of the Legendary Black Players and All-Black Professional Teams*. Oxford: Oxford University Press, 1992. 406 pp., includes index, paperback $15.95. ISBN 0-195-07637-0. A history of the legendary Black players and all-Black

professional teams. The author traces the history of Blacks in baseball and highlights the achievements of outstanding and legendary players.

399. Ritchie, Andrew. *Major Taylor: The Extraordinary Career of a Champion Bicycle Racer*. Baltimore, MD: Johns Hopkins University Press, 1996. 431 pp., paperback $16.95. ISBN 0-801-85303-6. This book details the qualities and life of a great bicyclist. Ritchie's narrative is designed bring Major Taylor's bicycling achievements to the attention of youth aspiring to a career in athletics.

400. Rodman, Dennis. *Bad as I Wanna Be*. New York: Delacorte Press, 1996. 259 pp., hardcover $22.95, paperback $6.99. ISBN 0-385-31639-9 (H), 0-440-22266-4 (P). Rodman, an NBA player, speaks candidly about his personal life and professional career. He covers everything from his childhood, a fling with Madonna, living in Oklahoma, to his entrance into the NBA. This honest memoir is at times shocking but always interesting. Rodman also includes photographs.

401. Rodman, Dennis. *Walk on the Wild Side*. New York: Delacorte Press, 1997. 224 pp., hardcover $22.95. ISBN 0-385-31897-9. Rodman's rebounding skills may only be surpassed by his outrageousness. *Walk on the Wild Side* is Rodman's thoughtful offering on a wide range of subjects from race and sex to politics. This book includes many personal anecdotes.

402. Rodman, Dennis, Rich, Pat, and Steinberg, Alan. *Rebound: The Enduring Friendship of Dennis Rodman and Bryne Rich*. New York: Crown, 1994. 246 pp., hardcover $22.00. ISBN 0-517-59294-0. This is a personal narrative from Rodman about his life and important friendship with Bryne Rich. It includes discussions about his career, early life, and life with the Rich family. Co-authored by Rich and Steinberg, *Rebound* shares many intimate stories and details about his personal life.

403. Rogosin, Donn. *Invisible Men: Life in Baseball's Negro Leagues*. New York: Atheneum, 1995. 283 pp., includes index, paperback $14.00. ISBN 1-568-36085-1. This book is based on five years of research, including interviews with virtually every surviving Negro League player. It gives a history of the Negro League and its players, along with stories about first class baseball, gamblers, exotic travel, big money, racism, and more.

404. Rosaforte, Tim. *Tiger Woods: The Making of a Champion*. New York: St. Martin's Press, 1997. Hardcover $21.95, paperback $5.99. ISBN 0-312-

15672-3 (H), 0-312-96437-4 (P). Rosaforte's book is a "behind the scenes" investigation into the phenomenon that is Tiger Woods. He examines what led to Tiger's success as he covers his training, upbringing and career.

405. Ruck, Rob. *Sandlot Seasons: Sport in Black Pittsburgh.* Chicago: University of Illinois Press, 1987. 238 pp., includes bibliography and index, paperback $21.95. ISBN 0-252-01322-0 (H), 0-252-06342-2 (P). In this revised dissertation, Ruck focuses on Black sports and their connection to the community. His specific focus is on sandlot baseball and football. Ruck also gives attention to the importance of sports, their connection to politics, and gambling. An excellent history of community sports.

406. Rust, Art, Jr. *"Get That Nigger Off the Field!": An Oral History of Black Ballplayers from the Negro Leagues to the Present.* New York: Delacorte Press, 1992. 228 pp., includes index, $7.95. ISBN 0-912-33119-4. The first total history of the Black baseball player, from the days of the Black Leagues through today. The author combines his memories as a young Black fan in the 1930s and 1940s, with the memories of famous Black players.

407. Sheed, Wilfred. *Muhammad Ali: A Portrait in Words and Photographs.* New York: Crowell, 1975. 254 pp. ISBN 0-690-00958-5. Sheed provides a biography of Muhammad Ali, perhaps the greatest athlete of our time. He includes photographs as he details Ali's life and fights as well as the constant media attention given to him.

408. Smith, Sam. *Second Coming: The Strange Odyssey of Michael Jordan from Courtside to Home Plate and Back Again.* New York: Harper Collins Publishers, 1995. 363 pp., paperback $5.99. ISBN 0-061-09455-2. This book details Jordan's return to the Chicago Bulls after his brief retirement. Smith addresses the impact of Jordan's comeback on the team, league, and Chicago.

409. Strege, John. *Tiger: A Biography of Tiger Woods.* New York: Broadway Books, 1997. 252 pp., hardcover $25.00, paperback $12.00. ISBN 0-553-06219-0 (H), 0-767-90145-2 (P). Strege, a reporter, takes the reader behind the scenes of golf. A longtime friend of the family, he chronicles Woods' evolution and success. Strege reveals that Woods has created a new audience for golf.

410. Tygiel, Jules. *Baseball's Great Experiment: Jackie Robinson and His Legacy*. New York: Oxford University Press, 1997. 413 pp., includes bibliography and index, paperback $16.95. ISBN 0-195-10619-9 (H), 0-195-10620-2 (P). In commemoration of the 50th anniversary of Jackie Robinson's entrance into baseball, Tygiel revised and expanded an earlier version of this text. The author draws on interviews with players and executives, newspaper accounts, and personal papers in this account of Jackie Robinson's influence on baseball and American culture.

411. Walker, Chet with Messenger, Chris. *Long Time Coming: A Black Athlete's Coming-of-Age in America*. New York: Grove Press, 1995. 258 pp. ISBN 0-802-11504-7. Chet Walker's memoir covers his childhood poverty and the racism he confronted on his rise to national prominence as a basketball player. He tells of the perseverance that a Black athlete has to possess in order to become a success.

412. White, Solomon with Schlichter, H. Walter (ed.). *Sol White's Official Baseball Guide*. Columbia, SC: Camden House, 1984. 128 pp. ISBN 0-848-81588-2. This is a reproduction of White's rare manuscript. The book gives a detailed look at Black baseball during the late 1800s and early 1900s. This book is rare in that it may be one of the only primary resources directly from the era describing the Negro leagues and their players.

413. Woods, Earl with McDaniel, Pete. *Training a Tiger: A Father's Guide to Raising a Winner in Both Golf and Life*. New York: Harper Collins, 1997. 239 pp., includes photos and illustrations, hardcover $19.95, paperback $5.99. ISBN 0-06-270178-9 (H), 0-06-101326-9 (P). Woods, father of golf favorite Tiger Woods, shares his philosophy of golf and life in general. He provides clues and illustrations for beginning golfers ranging from etiquette to technique. Earl also explains how he managed to raise a "winner." He weaves throughout the selection accounts of Tiger's rise to golf super-stardom.

414. Zang, David W. *Fleet Walker's Divided Heart: The Life of Baseball's First Black Major Leaguer*. Lincoln: University of Nebraska Press, 1995. 157 pp., includes bibliography and illustrations, hardcover $21.50, paperback $12.95. ISBN 0-8032-4913-6 (H), 0-8032-9913-3 (P). Zang has produced an account of Moses Fleetwood Walker, the first African-American to play in the international Baseball League. He addresses racism and the frustrations that hounded him throughout this life as he shares Walker's experiences.

15

Selected Works on the African-American Male

415. Abron, J. (1990). "The Image of African-Americans in the U.S. Press," *The Black Scholar, 21*(2), 49-52.

416. Aikens, C. (1971). "The Struggle of Curt Flood," *The Black Scholar, 3*(3), 10-15.

417. Akbar, N. *Visions for Black Men.* Tallahassee, FL: Mind Productions and Associates, 1991.

418. Allen, E., Jr. (1991/92). "Race and Gender Stereotyping in the Thomas Confirmation Hearings," *The Black Scholar, 22*(1-2), 13-15.

419. Allen, M. (1972). "The Case of Billy Dean Smith," *The Black Scholar, 4*(2), 15-17.

420. Allen, R.L. (1995). "Racism, Sexism and a Million Men," *The Black Scholar, 25*(4), 24-26.

421. Allen, W.R. (1978). "The Search for Applicable Theories of Black Family Life," *Journal of Marriage and Family, 40,* 117-129.

422. Allen, W.R. (1981). "Moms, Dads and Boys: Race and Sex Difference in the Socialization of Male Children," in Gary, Lawrence E. (ed.), *Black Men*. Beverly Hills, CA: Sage Publications.

423. Als, H. (1993). "The Malcomized Moment: En-gendering and Re-politicizing the X Man," *The Black Scholar, 23*(3-4), 24-38.

424. Alston, D.N. and Williams, N. (1982). "Relationship Between Father Absence and Self-Concept of Black Adolescent Boys," *The Journal of Negro Education, 51*(2), 134-138.

425. Anderson, E. (1989). "Sex Codes and Family Life Among Poor Inner-City Youths," *ANNALS, AAPSS, 501,* 59-78.

426. Anderson, M. (1993). "Studying Across Difference: Race, Class, and Gender in Qualitative Research," in Stanfield, J. and Dennis, R. (eds.), *Race and Ethnicity in Research Methods*, pg. 39-52. Newbury Park, CA: Sage Publications.

427. Andrews, William L. (1994). "The Black Male in American Literature," in Majors, Richard G. and Gordon, Jacob U. (eds.), *The American Black Male: His Past, Present, and Future*, pg. 60-68. Chicago: Nelson-Hall.

428. Asante, Molefi K. (1981). "Black Male and Female Relationships: An Afrocentric Context," in Gary, Lawrence E. (ed.), *Black Men.* Beverly Hills, CA: Sage Publications.

429. Asante, Molefi and Davis, A. (1985). "Black and White Communication: Analyzing Work Place Encounters," *Journal of Black Studies, 16*(1), 77-93.

430. Ashe, Arthur (1989). "Is Proposition 42 Racist? No!," *Ebony, 44,* 138-140.

431. Austin, Bobby (ed.). *A Discussion of Issues Affecting African-American Men and Boys*. Battle Creek, MI: W.K. Kellogg Foundation, 1992.

432. Barnes, A.S. *Retention of African-American Males in High School: A Study of African-American Male High School Dropouts, African-American Male Seniors, and White Male Seniors*. Lanham, MD: University Press of America, 1992.

433. Bell, C.C., Prothrow-Stith, D., Smallwood, C.S., and Murchison, C. (1986). "Black-on-Black Homicide: The National Medical Association's Responsibilities," *Journal of the National Medical Association, 78,* 139-141.

434. Biller, H.B. (1969). "A Note on Father Absence and Masculine Development in Young Lower-Class Negro and White Boys," *Child Development, 39,* 1003-1006.

435. Biller, H.B., and Borstelmann, L. (1967). "Masculine Development: An Integrative View," *Merrill-Palmer Quarterly, 13,* 253-94.

436. *The Black Scholar* (1991). "Port Chicago Case Comes Before U.S. Congress," *21*(3), 38-39.

437. Block, J.H. (1973). "Conceptions of Sex Role: Some Cross-Cultural and Longitudinal Perspectives," *American Psychologist, 28,* 512-520.

438. Bond, J.C. and Peery, P. (1970). "Is the Black Male Castrated?" in Cade, Toni (ed.), *The Black Woman: An Anthology,* pg. 113-118. New York: Signet.

439. *Boule Journal.* The official publication (1904-present) of the Sigma Pi Phi Fraternity, 920 Broadway, Suite 703, New York, NY 10010.

440. Bowman, P.J. (1985). "Black Fathers and the Provider Role: Role Strain, Informal Coping Resource and Life Happiness," in Boykin, A.W. (ed.), *Empirical Research in Black Psychology,* pg. 9-19. Washington, DC: National Institute for Mental Health.

441. Bowman, P.J. (1989). "Research Perspectives on Black Men: Role Strain and Adaptation Across the Adult Life Cycle," in Jones, R.L. (ed.), *Black Adult Development and Aging.* Berkeley, CA: Cobbs and Henry.

442. Bowman, P.J. and Howard, C. (1985). "Race-Related Socialization, Motivation, and Academic Achievement: A Study of Black Youths in Three-Generation Families," *Journal of the American Academy of Child Psychiatry, 24*(2), 134-141.

443. Boyd, M.J. (1991/92). "Collard Greens, Clarence Thomas, and the High-tech Rape of Anita Hill," *The Black Scholar, 22*(1-2), 25-27.

444. Braddock, J.H. and McPartland, J.M. (1987). "How Minorities Continue to be Excluded From Equal Employment Opportunities: Research on Labor Market and Institutional Barriers," *Journal of Social Issues, 43*(1), 5-39.

445. Bradley, R.H., Rock, S.L., Caldwell, B.M., Harris, P.T., and Hamrick, H.M. (1987). "Home Environment and School Performance Among Black Elementary School Children," *Journal of Negro Education, 56*(4), 499-509.

446. Braithwaite, R.L. (1981). "Interpersonal Relations Between Black Males and Black Families," in Gary, Lawrence E. (ed.), *Black Men.* Beverly Hills, CA: Sage Publications.

447. Brim, O.G., Jr. (1976). "Theories of the Male Mid-Life Crisis," *The Counseling Psychologist, 6,* 2-9.

448. Brimmer, A.F. (1984). "Long-term Economic Growth and Black Employment Opportunities," *The Review of Black Political Economy, 13*(3), 5-19.

449. Broder, J.M. (1995, October 13). "Planned March Turns Into Debate Over Support for Farrakhan," *Los Angeles Times* (on-line).

450. Brown, W.W. (1971). "A Pioneer Black Historian and Nat Turner," in Foner, Eric (ed.), *Nat Turner,* pg. 141-145. Englewood Cliffs, NJ: Prentice-Hall.

451. Bruce, Marino A., Roscigno, Vincent J., and McCall, Patricia L. (1998). "Structure, Context and Agency in the Reproduction of Black-on-Black Violence," *Theoretical Criminology, 2,* 29-55.

452. Carroll, A. (1970, July). "On Illegitimate Capitalist 'The Game,'" *The Black Panther.*

453. Carter, Lawrence Edward. *The Crisis of the African-American Male: Dangers and Opportunities.* Beckham House Publishing, 1995.

454. Cazenave, N.A. (1983). "Black Male-Female Relationships: The Perceptions of 155 Middle-Class Black Men," *Family Relations, 32,* 341-350.

455. Cazenave, N.A. (1981). "Black Men in America: The Quest for Manhood," in McAdoo, H.P. (ed.), *Black Families*. Beverly Hills, CA: Sage Publications.

456. Cazenave, N.A. (1979). "Middle-Income Black Fathers: An Analysis of the Provider Role," *The Family Coordinator, 28*, 583-593.

457. Cazenave, N.A. (1984). "Race, Socioeconomic Status, and Age: The Social Context of American Masculinity," *Sex Roles, 11*(7/8), 639-656.

458. Centers, R., Raven, B.H., and Rodrigues, A. (1971, April). "Conjugal Power Structure: A Re-examination," *American Sociological Review, 36*, 264-278.

459. Cicone, M.V. and Ruble, D.N. (1978). "Beliefs About Males," *Journal of Social Issues, 34*(1), 5-16.

460. *CNN* (1995, October 16). "Behind Million Men, Black Women--'No Girls Allowed' Request Leaves Community Divided," (CNN Interactive).

461. *CNN* (1995, October 17). "Minister Farrakhan Challenges Black Men," Transcript from Minister Louis Farrakhan's remarks at the Million Man March (CNN Interactive).

462. Cokley, K. (1996). "The Psychological and Sociohistorical Antecedents of Violence: An Afrocentric Analysis," *Journal of African-American Men, 2*(1), 3-14.

463. Cole, Maria. *Nat King Cole: An Intimate Biography*. New York: W. Morrow, 1971.

464. Crawley, B. and Freeman, E.M. (1993). "Themes in the Life Views of Older and Younger African-American Males," *Journal of African-American Male Studies, 1*(1), 15-29.

465. *The Crisis* (1986). "Black Males in Jeopardy?" *93*, 1-47.

466. Cunningham, M. (1993). "Sex Role Influences of African-American Males: A Literature Review," *Journal of African-American Male Studies, 1*(1), 30-37.

467. Cuyjet, Michael J. (ed.). *Helping African-American Men Succeed in College* (New Directions for Student Services, No. 80). San Francisco: Jossey-Bass, 1998.

468. Dales, R. and Keller, J. (1972). "Self-Concept Scores Among Black and White Culturally Deprived Adolescent Males," *Journal of Negro Education, 41,* 31-34.

469. Daniels, L.A. (1995, February). "The American Way: Blame a Black Man," *Emerge,* 60-62, 64, 66, 68.

470. Datcher, L. (1980). "Effects of Community, Family, and Education on the Earnings of Black and White Men," *The Review of Black Political Economy, 10,* 291-394.

471. Davenport, D. and Yurich, J. (1991). "Multicultural Gender Issues," *Journal of Counseling and Development, 70*(1), 64.

472. Davis, F.M. *Livin' the Blues: Memoirs of a Black Journalist and Poet.* Madison, WI: University of Wisconsin Press, 1992.

473. Davis, R. (1981). "A Demographic Analysis of Suicide," in Gary, Lawrence E. (ed.), *Black Men.* Beverly Hills, CA: Sage Publications.

474. Dawsey, Darrell. *Living to Tell About It: Young Black Men in America Speak Their Piece.* New York: Anchor Books, 1996.

475. Documentary Sources Database (1996). Copy of a letter from Benjamin Banneker, American Multiculturalism Series, Unit One. *Documenting the African-American Experience.* Charlottesville: University of Virginia Library Electronic Text Center. Printed by Daniel Lawrence, no. 33. North Fourth-Street. Philadelphia [1792]. Early American Imprints, 1st Series, no. 24073.

476. Dorr, R. (1982). "Television and the Socialization of the Minority Child," in Berry, G.L. and Mitchell-Kernan, C. (eds.), *Television and the Socialization of the Minority Child.* New York: Academic Press.

477. DuBois, W.E.B. (1902). "Of the Training of Black Men," *Atlantic Monthly, 90,* 289-297.

478. DuBois, W.E.B. (1918, July). "Close Ranks," *The Crisis, 16,* 111.

479. DuBois, W.E.B. (1961). "Of Mr. Booker T. Washington and Others," in *The Souls of Black Folk*. New York: Fawcett Publications.

480. DuBois, W.E.B. (1971). "An History Toward a History of the Black Man in the Great War," in Lester, J. (ed.), *The Seventh Son: The Thought and Writings of W.E.B. Du Bois* (Volume 2), pg. 130-131. New York: Random House.

481. Durnell, N.Y. (1993). "National News Magazine's Portrayal of the Reverend Jesse Louis Jackson as a Mythical Hero During the 1988 United States Presidential Campaign, National News Magazine," *National News Magazine*.

482. Earl, J. and Lohmann, M. (1978) "Absent Fathers and Black Male Children," *Social Work, 23,* 413-415.

483. Edwards, H. (1971). "The Sources of the Black Athlete's Superiority," *The Black Scholar, 3*(3), 32-41.

484. Elliot, J.M. (1993, August 23/30). "The Willie Horton Nobody Knows," *The Nation,* 201-205.

485. Equiano, Olaudah (1987). "The Interesting Narrative of the Life of Olaudah Equiano, or Gustavus Vassa, the African," in Gates, Henry Louis, Jr. (ed.), *The Classic Slave Narratives*. New York: Penguin. (Originally published in 1814 by Leeds.)

486. Farrakhan, Louis (1995). "Allah (God) Hates Divorce--Part Two," *The Final Call, 14*(18). (Available on the Nation of Islam web site, http://www.noi.org, listed under Resources--Articles and Speeches by Minister Louis Farrakhan.)

487. Farrakhan, Louis (1995). "Minister Louis Farrakhan Speaks on Domestic Violence," *The Final Call, 14*(20), 1-3.

488. Fendrich, J. (1972). "Returning Black Vietnam Era Veterans," *Social Service Review, 46,* 60-75.

489. Ferguson, R.F. (1991). "Racial Patterns in How School and Teacher Quality Affect Achievement and Earnings," *Challenge: A Journal of Research on Black Men, 2*(1), 1-35.

490. Ferguson, R.F. (1994). "How Professionals in Community-Based Programs Perceive and Respond to the Needs of Black Male Youth," in Mincy, Ronald B. (ed.), *Nurturing Young Black Males: Challenges to Agencies, Programs, and Social Policy*. Washington, DC: The Urban Institute Press.

491. Fleming, J.E. (1981). "Black Males in Higher Education," in Gary, Lawrence E. (ed.), *Black Men*. Beverly Hills, CA: Sage Publications.

492. Foner, Eric (ed.). *Nat Turner*. Englewood Cliffs, NJ: Prentice-Hall, 1971.

493. Fordham, S. (1988). "Racelessness as a Factor in Black Students' School Success: Pragmatic Strategy or Pyrrhic Victory?" *Harvard Educational Review, 58*(1), 54-84.

494. Fordham, S. and Ogbu, J.U. (1986). "Black Students' School Success: Coping with the 'Burden of Acting White,'" *The Urban Review, 18*(3), 176-206.

495. Francis, C.E. *The Tuskegee Airmen: The Men Who Changed a Nation*. Boston: Branden Pub. Co., 1993.

496. Franklin, C.W. (1986). "Conceptual and Logical Issues in Theory and Research Related to Black Masculinity," *The Western Journal of Black Studies, 10*(4), 161-165.

497. Garibaldi, A.M. (1991). "The Educational Experiences of Black Males: The Early Years," *Challenge: A Journal of Research on Black Men, 2*(1), 36-49.

498. Gary, Lawrence E. (1985). "Depressive Symptoms and Black Men," *Social Work Research and Abstracts, 21*(4), 21-29.

499. Gary, Lawrence E. (1986). "Family Life Events, Depression and Black Men," in Lewis, R.A. and Salt, R.E. (eds.), *Men in Families*, pg. 215-231. Beverly Hills, CA: Sage Publications.

500. Gary, Lawrence E., Booker, C.B., and Fekade, A. *African-American Males: An Analysis of Contemporary Values, Attitudes, and Perceptions of Manhood*. Final Report. Washington, DC: School of Social Work, Howard University, 1993.

501. Gatewood, W.B., Jr. (ed.). *Free Men of Color: The Autobiography of Willis Augustus Hodges*. Knoxville: The University of Tennessee Press, 1982.

502. Gayle, A. *Oak and Ivy: A Biography of Paul Laurence Dunbar*. Garden City, NY: Doubleday, 1971.

503. Ghee, K.L. (1990). "Enhancing Educational Achievement Through Cultural Awareness in Young Black Males," *The Western Journal of Black Studies, 14*(2), 77-89.

504. Gibbs, J.T. (1988). "Health and Mental Health of Young Black Males," in Gibbs, J.T. (ed.), *Black, Young, and Male in America: An Endangered Species*. Dover, MA: Auburn House.

505. Goddard, L.L. (ed.). *An African-Centered Model of Prevention for African-American Youth at High Risk*. Rockville, MD: Substance Abuse and Mental Health Services Administration, Center for Substance Abuse Prevention, 1993.

506. Goff, S. and Sanders, R. *Brothers: Black Soldiers in the Nam*. New York: Berkley Books, 1982.

507. Gorn, E.J. (ed.). *Muhammad Ali, the People's Champ*. Urbana: University of Illinois Press, 1995.

508. Govan, M. (1971). "The Emergence of the Black Athlete in America," *The Black Scholar, 3*(3), 16-28.

509. Greene, L.J. *Working With Carter G. Woodson, the Father of Black History: A Diary, 1928-1930*. Baton Rouge: Louisiana State University Press, 1989.

510. Gutman, B. *Magic, More Than a Legend: A Biography*. New York: Harper Paperbacks, 1992.

511. Hahn, A.B. (1994). "Toward a National Youth Development Policy for Young African-American Males: The Choices Policymakers Face," in Mincy, Ronald B. (ed.), *Nurturing Young Black Males: Challenges to Agencies, Programs, and Social Policy*. Washington, DC: Urban Institute Press.

512. Hale, Janice E. *Unbank the Fire: Visions for the Education of African-American Children.* Baltimore, MD: Johns Hopkins University Press, 1994.

513. Hall, L.K. (1981). "Support Systems and Coping Patterns," in Gary, Lawrence E. (ed.), *Black Men.* Beverly Hills, CA: Sage Publications.

514. Hammond, J. and Enoch, J.R. (1976). "Conjugal Power Relations Among Black Working Class Families," *Journal of Black Studies, 7*(1), 107-127.

515. Hanley, S. *A. Phillip Randolph.* New York: Chelsea House Publishers, 1989.

516. Hardy, James Earl. *Boyz II Men.* New York: Chelsea House Publishers, 1996.

517. Hare, B.R. (1987). "Structural Inequality and the Endangered Status of Black Youth," *Journal of Negro Education, 56,* 100-110.

518. Hare, Nathan (1971). "The Frustrated Masculinity of the Negro Male," in Staples, Robert (ed.), *The Black Family.* Belmont, CA: Wadsworth Publishing Company.

519. Hare, Nathan (1971). "A Study of the Black Fighter," *The Black Scholar, 3*(3), 2-9.

520. Hare, Nathan (1971). "Will the Real Black Man Please Stand Up?" *The Black Scholar, 2*(10), 32-35.

521. Hare, Nathan (1978). "Revolution Without a Revolution: The Psychosociology of Sex and Race," *The Black Scholar, 9*(7), 2-7.

522. Hartley, R. (1959). "Sex-Role Pressures in the Socialization of the Male Child," *Psychological Reports, 5,* 457-468.

523. Haskins, James. *A Piece of the Power: Four Black Mayors.* New York: Dial Press, 1972.

524. Haskins, James. *Always Movin' On: The Life of Langston Hughes.* Trenton, NJ: Africa World Press, 1993.

525. Haskins, James. *Diary of a Harlem Schoolteacher.* New York: Grove Press, 1969.

526. Hatcher, W.E. *John Jasper: The Unmatched Negro Philosopher and Preacher*. New York: Negro Universities Press, 1969.

527. Haw, K. (1991). "Interactions of Gender and Race--A Problem for Teachers? A Review of the Emerging Literature," *Educational Research, 33*(1), 12.

528. Hawkins, D.F. (ed.), *Homicide among Black Americans*. Lanham, MD: University Press of America, 1986.

529. Hawkins, D.F. (1983). "Black and White Homicide Differentials: Alternative to an Inadequate Theory," *Criminal Justice Behavior, 10,* 407-40.

530. Hawkins, Walter L. *African-American Biographies: Profiles of 558 Current Men and Women*. Jefferson, NC: McFarland & Co, 1992.

531. Hayman, C.R. and Probst, J.C. (1983). "Health Status of Disadvantaged Adolescents Entering the Job Corps Program," *Public Health Reports, 98,* 369-376.

532. Hays, W. and Mindel, C. (1973). "Extended Kinship Relations in Black and White Families," *Journal of Marriage and Family, 35,* 51-57.

533. Hendricks, L.E. (1981). "Black Unwed Adolescent Fathers," in Gary, L.E. (Ed.), *Black Men*, pg. 131-38. Beverly Hills, CA: Sage Publications.

534. Henry, C.P. (1981). "The Political Role of the 'Bad Nigger,'" *The Black Scholar, 11*(4), 461-482.

535. Hetherington, E. (1966). "Effects of Paternal Adolescence on Sex-Typed Behavior in Negro and White Males," *Journal of Personality and Social Psychology, 4,* 87-91.

536. Hill, R.B. (1988). "Adolescent Male Responsibility in African-American Families," paper delivered to the National Urban League Conference on "Manhood and Fatherhood: Adolescent Male Responsibility in Black Families." March 20-22, Atlanta, GA.

537. Hopkins, T. (1973). "The Role of the Agency in Supporting Black Manhood," *Social Work, 18,* 53-58.

538. Hrabowski, Freeman A., Maton, Kenneth I., and Greif, Geoffrey L. *Beating the Odds: Raising Academically Successful African-American Males*. New York: Oxford University Press, 1998.

539. Hubert, J.M. *Bogun, The Slave Stud*. New York: Vintage Press, 1984.

540. Hunter, A.G. and Davis, J.E. (1992). "Constructing Gender: An Exploration of Afro-American Men's Conceptualization of Manhood," *Gender and Society, 6*(3), 464-479.

541. Hutchinson, Earl Ofari. *Black Fatherhood II: Black Women Talk About Their Men*. Los Angeles: Middle Passage Press, 1994.

542. Jackson, Edward M. *Images of Black Men in Black Women Writers, 1950-1990*. Bristol, IN: Wyndham Hall Press, 1993.

543. Jackson, G. (1971). "Struggle and the Black Man," *The Black Scholar, 2*(10), 48-52.

544. Jackson, J. (1974). "Ordinary Black Husbands-Fathers: The Truly Hidden Men," *Journal of Social and Behavioral Sciences, 20,* 19-27.

545. Jackson, J. (1978). "But Where Are the Men?" in Staples, Robert (ed.), *The Black Family: Essays and Studies*. Belmont, CA: Wadsworth Publishing Company.

546. Jackson-Leslie, L. (1992). "Tom, Buck, and Sambo or How Clarence Thomas Got to the Supreme Court," *The Black Scholar, 22*(1-2), 52-54.

547. James, P.P. (1989). "Hubert H. Harrison and the New Negro Movement," *Western Journal of Black Studies, 13*(2), 82-91.

548. Jarrett, H. *The History of Sigma Pi Phi, Vol. II*. Philadelphia: Quantum Leap Publishers, Inc., 1995.

549. Jeff, M.X., Jr. (1994). "Afrocentrism and African-American Male Youths," in Mincy, Ronald B. (ed.), *Nurturing Young Black Males: Challenges to Agencies, Programs, and Social Policy*. Washington, DC: The Urban Institute Press.

550. Jiobu, R.M. (1988). "Racial Inequality in a Public Arena: The Case of Professional Baseball," *Social Forces, 67,* 524-534.

551. Johnson, C. (1993). "Television Commercials: The Social and Economic Implications for Men of Color," *Journal of African-American Male Studies, 1*(1), 47-55.

552. Johnson, Ernest H. *Brothers on the Mend: Understanding and Healing for African-American Men and Women.* New York: Pocket Books, 1998.

553. Johnson, J. (1989). "Is Proposition 42 Racist? Yes!," *Ebony, 44,* 138-40.

554. Johnson, Jack. *Jack Johnson in the Ring and Out.* Chicago: National Sports Publishing Company, 1927.

555. Johnson, Jack. *Jack Johnson is a Dandy: An Autobiography.* New York: Chelsea House, 1969.

556. Johnson, L. and Staples, R. (1979). "Family Planning and the Young Minority Male: A Pilot Project," *The Family Coordinator, 28,* 535-43.

557. Johnson, R.E., Marcos, A.C., and Bahr, S.J. (1987). "The Role of Peers in the Complex Etiology of Adolescent Drug Use," *Criminology, 25*(2), 323-340.

558. Jones, C.A. (1993). "Academic Achievement and Retention in an Educational Program Exclusive to African-American Males," *Journal of African-American Male Studies, 1*(2), 87-91.

559. Jones, Dionne J. *African-American Males: A Critical Link in the African-American Family.* New Brunswick, NJ: Transaction Publishers, 1994.

560. Jones, R.S. (1993). "Double Burdens, Double Responsibilities: Eighteenth-Century Black Males and the African-American Struggle," *Journal of African-American Male Studies, 1*(1), 1-14.

561. *Journal of African-American Men.* A publication of the National Council of African-American Men. Transaction Periodical Consortium, Rutgers University, New Brunswick, NJ.

562. Karenga, R. (1972). "Overturning Ourselves: From Mystification to Meaningful Struggle," *The Black Scholar, 4*(2), 6-14.

563. Key, William J. and Smith, Robert Johnson (eds.). *From one Brother to Another: Voices of African American Men.* Valley Forge, PA: Judson Press, 1996.

564. Kimmel, Michael S. (ed.). *Changing Men: New Directions in Research on Men and Masculinity.* Newbury Park, CA: Sage Publications, 1987.

565. King, D.K. (1992). "Unraveling Fabric, Missing the Beat: Class and Gender in Afro-American Social Issues," *The Black Scholar, 22*(3), 36-44.

566. King, Martin Luther, Jr. (1975). "A Time to Break Silence," in Foner, P.S. (Ed.), *The Voice of Black America* (Volume two). New York: Capricorn Books.

567. King, Martin Luther, Jr. *Where do We Go from Here: Chaos or Community?* New York: Harper & Row, 1967.

568. Knapp, G.E. *Buffalo Soldiers at Fort Leavenworth in the 1930s and Early 1940s.* Fort Leavenworth, KS: Combat Studies Institute, 1991.

569. Langston, J.M. *From the Virginia Plantation to the National Capitol or the First and Only Negro Representative in Congress from the Old Dominion.* Hartford, CT: American Publishing Company, 1894.

570. Larabee, M. (1986). "Helping Reluctant Black Males: An Affirmative Approach," *Journal of Multicultural Counseling and Development, 14,* 25-37.

571. Lewis, D.K. (1975). "The Black Family: Socialization and Sex Roles," *Phylon, 36*(3), 221-237.

572. Locy, T. (1996, March 28). "'Deplorable' Unit Alleged at DC Jail," *The Washington Post*, pg. A1, A15.

573. Lucas, J. *Winning a Day at a Time.* Center City, MN.: Hazelden, 1994.

574. Lunardini, C. (1980). "Standing Firm: William Monroe Trotter's Meetings with Woodrow Wilson, 1913-1914," *Journal of Negro History, xx,* 244-264.

575. Lynch, J.P. and Sabol, W.J. (1994, November 9). "The Use of Coercive Social Control and Changes in the Race and Class Composition of U.S. Prison Populations," paper presented at the American Society of Criminology.

576. MacOn, Larry L. *Discipling the African-American Male: How to Get Black Men into Church and Keep them There.* Nashville, TN: Winston-Derek Publishing, 1997.

577. Madhubuti, Haki R. *Developmental Manual for Young Black Males.* Chicago: Third World Press, 1996.

578. Majors, Richard (1989). "Cool Pose: The Proud Signature of Black Survival," in Messner, M. and Kimmel, M. (eds.), *Men's Lives: Readings in the Sociology of Men and Masculinity.* New York: Macmillan Publishing Company.

579. Majors, Richard (1989). "Cool Pose: Black Masculinity and Sports," in Messner, M. and Sabo, D. (eds.), *Sports, Men, and the Gender Order: Critical Feminist Perspectives.* Champaign, IL: Human Kinestics.

580. Majors, Richard (1991). "Nonverbal Behaviors and Communication Styles Among African-Americans," in Jones, R.L. (ed.), *Black Psychology* (3rd Edition). Berkeley, CA: Cobb and Henry.

581. Malin, B.T. *An Introduction to Research on the Developmental Needs of Young Black Males.* Washington, DC: Joint Center for Political and Economic Studies, 1994.

582. Malveaux, J. (1986). "Review of the Impact of Cybernation Technology on Black Automotive Workers in the United States," *The Review of Black Political Economy, 15*(1), 103-5.

583. Matsueda, R.L. and Heimer, K. (1987). "Race, Family Structure, and Delinquency: A Test of Differential Association and Social Control Theories," *American Sociological Review, 57,* 826-840.

584. Mauer, M. and Haling, T. *Young Black Americans and the Criminal Justice System: Five Years Later.* Washington, DC: The Sentencing Project, 1995.

585. McAdoo, J.L. (1981). "Black Father and Child Interaction," in Gary, Lawrence E. (ed.), *Black Men.* Beverly Hills, CA: Sage Publications.

586. McPherson, J.M. *The Negro's Civil War: How Many Blacks Felt and Acted During the War for the Union.* New York: Ballantine Books, 1991.

587. Means, H.B. *Colin Powell: Soldier/Statesman--Statesman/Soldier.* New York: D.I. Fine, 1992.

588. Mellon, J. (ed.). *Bullwhip Days: The Slaves Remember, an Oral History.* New York: Avon Books, 1988.

589. Miller, Chris M. (1996). "The Representation of the Black Male in Film," *Chris Miller's Home Page,* http://gti.net/cmmiller/.

590. Mincy, Ronald B. (1991). "*Workforce 2000,* Silver Bullet or Dud: Job Structure Changes and Economic Prospects for Black Males in the 1990s," *Challenge: A Journal of Research on Black Males, 2*(1), 50-76.

591. Moreland, J. (1980). "Age and Change in the Adult Male Sex Role," *Sex Roles, 6,* 807-818.

592. Morris, E.C. *Sermons, Addresses, and Reminiscences, and Important Correspondence.* New York: Arno Press, 1980.

593. Muhammad, A.A. (1995). "Black Woman, This March is for You," *The Final Call 14*(22).

594. Murray, C.B., Smith, S.N. and West, E.H. (1989). "Comparative Personality Development in Adolescence: A Critique," in Jones, R.L. (ed.), *Black Adolescents,* pg. 49-62. Berkeley, CA: Cobb and Henry.

595. *National African-American Male Collaboration Journal.* First issue to be published in 2000. National African-American Male Collaboration, Hull House Association, 10 South Riverside Plaza, Chicago, IL, 60606. Phone 312-906-8600, fax 312-906-8822, and email naamc@aol.com.

596. Newton, Huey P. (1968, March 16). "Executive Mandate No. 3," *The Black Panther.*

597. Nobles, Wade W. (1974). "Africanity: Its Role in Black Families," *The Black Scholar, 5*(9), 10-17.

598. Nobles, Wade W. (1978). "Toward an Empirical and Theoretical Framework for Defining Black Families," *Journal of Marriage and the Family, 40*(4), 679-687.

599. Nobles, Wade W. (1981). "African-American Family Life: An Instrument of Culture," in McAdoo, H.P. (ed.), *Black Families*, pg. 77-86. Beverly Hills, CA: Sage Publications.

600. Nobles, Wade W., Goddard, L., and Cavil, W. *Agenda for the 21st Century: A Strategic Plan for the Empowerment of Black Men*. Oakland, CA: Institute for the Advanced Study of Black Family Life and Culture, Inc., (in press).

601. Norton, M.B., Gutman, H.G., and Berlin, I. (1983). "The Afro-American Family in the Age of Revolution," in Berlin, Ira and Hoffman, Ronald (eds.), *Slavery and Freedom in the Age of the American Revolution*, pg. 175-192. Charlottesville: University Press of Virginia.

602. Okwu, Julian C.R. *Face Forward: Young African-American Men in a Critical Age*. San Francisco: Chronicle Books, 1997.

603. Oliver, W. (1984). "Black Males and the Tough Guy Image: A Dysfunctional Compensatory Adaptation," *The Western Journal of Black Studies, 8,* 199-202.

604. Oliver, W. (1989). "Black Males and Social Problems: Prevention Through Afrocentric Socialization," *Journal of Black Studies, 20*(1), 15-39.

605. Oliver, W. (1989). "Sexual Conquest and Patterns of Black-on-Black Violence: A Structural-Cultural Perspective," *Violence and Victims, 4*(4), 257-272.

606. Orlofsky, J. (1977). "Sex Role Orientation, Identity Formation and Self-Esteem in College Men and Women," *Sex Roles, 3,* 561-575.

607. Orr, James. *The Black Athlete: His Story in American History*. New York: Lion Books, 1969.

608. Osofsky, G. (ed.) (1967). "A View of the Negro as Beast," in *The Burden of Race: A Documentary History of Negro-White Relations in America*, pg. 184-187. New York: Harper Torchbooks.

609. Owens, Jesse with Neimark, P.G. *Jesse, The Man Who Outran Hitler*. New York: Fawcett Gold Medal, 1978.

610. Parham, T. and Williams, P. (1993). "The Relationship of Demographic and Background Factors to Racial Identity Attitudes," *Journal of Black Psychology, 19*(1), 7.

611. Parker, S. and Kleiner, R. J. (1969). "Social and Psychological Dimensions of the Family Role Performances of the Negro Male," *Journal of Marriage and the Family, 31,* 500-506.

612. Patton, J.M. (1981). "The Black Male's Struggle for an Education," in Gary, Lawrence E. (ed.), *Black Men.* Beverly Hills, CA: Sage Publications.

613. Payton, Walter with Jenkins, J. *Sweetness.* Chicago: Contemporary Books, 1978.

614. Pinn, A.B. (1996). "'Gettin' Grown': Notes on Gangsta Rap Music and Notions of Manhood," *Journal of African-American Men, 2*(1), 61-74.

615. Pittman, K.J. and Zeldin, S. (1994). "From Deterrence to Development: Shifting the Focus of Youth Programs for African-American Males," in Mincy, Ronald B. (ed.), *Nurturing Young Black Males: Challenges to Agencies, Programs, and Social Policy.* Washington, DC: The Urban Institute Press.

616. Polite, V.C. (1993). "Educating African-American Males in Suburbia: Quality Education . . . Caring Environment?" *Journal of African-American Male Studies, 1*(2), 92-105.

617. Poussaint, A.F. (1986). "Save the Fathers: They Must Regain Their Traditional Strengths," *Ebony, 41,* 43-50.

618. Proctor, Samuel D. *The Substance of Things Hoped For: A Memoir of African-American Faith.* New York: G.P. Putnam's Sons, 1995.

619. Pugh, T. and Mudd, E. (1971). "Attitudes of Black Women and Men Toward Using Community Services," *Journal of Religion and Health, 10*(3), 256-77.

620. Pullman, Wesley E. *African-American Men in Crisis: Proactive Strategies for Urban Youth.* New York: Garland Publishers, 1995.

621. Rainwater, L. (1965). "Crucible of Identity: The Negro Lower-Class Family," *Daedalus, 95,* 172-216.

622. Redkey, Edwin S. *A Grand Army of Black Men: Letters from African-American Soldiers in the Union Army, 1861-1865*. New York: Cambridge University Press, 1993.

623. Reed, I. (1989). "The Black Pathology Blitz," *The Nation, 249*(17), 597-598.

624. Reed, R.J. (1988). "Education and Achievement of Young Black Males," in Gibbs, J.W. (ed.), *Young, Black, and Male in America: An Endangered Species*. Dover, MA: Auburn Publishing Company.

625. Reef, Catherine. *Black Fighting Men: A Proud History*. New York: Twenty First Century Books, 1994.

626. Reid, P.T. (1985). "Sex-Role Socialization of Black Children: A Review of Theory, Family, and Media Influence," *Academic Psychology Bulletin, 7*(2), 201-212.

627. Reiser, H. *Scottie Pippin: Prince of the Court*. Chicago: Children's Press, 1993.

628. Rimmer, J. et al. (1971). "Alcoholism, Sex, Socioeconomic Status, and Race in Two Hospital Samples," *Quarterly Journal of Studies on Alcohol, 32*, 942-952.

629. Roosevelt, Theodore (1951). Letter to Dr. Lyman Abbott, October 29, 1903, in Morrison, E.E. (ed.), *The Letters of Theodore Roosevelt*, pg. 638-639. Cambridge, MA: Harvard University Press.

630. Roosevelt, Theodore (1951). Letter to Governor Winfield T. Durbin, August 6, 1903, in Morrison, E.E. (ed.), *The Letters of Theodore Roosevelt*, p. 1169. Cambridge, MA: Harvard University Press.

631. Ross, Marilyn J. *Success Factors of Young African-American Males at a Historically Black College*. Westport, CT: Bergin & Garvey, 1998.

632. Rowan, G.T. and Akers, T.A. (1996). "Technological Change and Organizational Differentiation in African-American Nonprofit Human Services," *Journal of African-American Men, 2*(1), 75-97.

633. Sabin, L. *The Fabulous Dr. J.: All Time All Star*. New York: Putnam, 1976.

634. Saunders, M. (1990, August). "Brothers-It Begins With Me," *Essence*, pg. 40.

635. Scott, J. (1976). "Polygamy: A Futuristic Family Arrangement for African-Americans," *Black Books Bulletin,* 13-19.

636. Scott, J.W. and Black, A. (1989). "Deep Structures of African-American Family Life: Female and Male Kin Networks," *The Western Journal of Black Studies, 13*(1), 17-24.

637. Seelow, D. (1996). "Look Forward in Anger: Young, Black Males and the New Cinema," *Journal of Men's Studies, 5*(2), 153-178.

638. The Sentencing Project (1990). "Black Males and the Criminal Justice System." Washington, DC.

639. Shabazz, Betty (1990). "Malcolm X as Husband and Father," in Clarke, J.H. (ed.), *Malcolm X: The Man and His Times*, pg. 132-143. Trenton, NJ: Africa World Press.

640. Shaw, Thomas M. *What Manner of Men: A Reconsideration Across the Synapses of Art History of Three Paintings and Their Images of Men of African Descent*. Lanham, MD: University Press of America, 1997.

641. Sifford, C. *Just Let Me Play: The Story of Charlie Sifford, The First Black Golfer*. Lanham, MD: University Press of America, 1992.

642. Singh, Robert. *The Congressional Black Caucus: Racial Politics in the U.S. Congress*. Thousand Oaks, CA: Sage Publications, 1998.

643. Smith, T. (1993, Summer). "Hyperactivity & Adolescent African-American Males," in *Berkeley McNair Journal,* v1, http://www-mcnair.berkeley.edu/uga/ost/mcnair.

644. Snell, W.E., Miller, R.S., Belk, S.S., Garcia-Falconi, R., and Hernandez-Sanchez, J. (1989). "Men's and Women's Emotional Disclosures: The Impact of Disclosure Recipient, Culture, and the Masculine Role," *Sex Roles, 21*(7-8), 467-485.

645. Spanier, G.B. and Glick, P.O. (1980). "Mate Selection Differentials Between Whites and Blacks in the United States," *Social Forces, 58*(4), 707-25.

646. Spence, J.T. (1984). "Masculinity, Femininity, and Gender-Related Traits: A Conceptual Analysis and Critique of Current Research," in Maher, B.A. and Maher, W.B. (eds.), *Progress in Experimental Personality Research* (Vol. 13). New York: Academic Press.

647. Staples, Robert (1971). "The Myth of the Impotent Black Male," *The Black Scholar, 2*(10), 2-9.

648. Staples, Robert (1971). "A Response to Clemmont Vontress," *The Black Scholar, 3*(3), 42-45.

649. Staples, Robert (1978). "Masculinity and Race: The Dual Dilemma of Black Men," *Journal of Social Issues, 34,* 169-183.

650. Staples, Robert (1978). "The Myth of Black Sexual Superiority: A Re-examination," *The Black Scholar, 9*(7), 16-22.

651. Staples, Robert (1979). "A Rejoinder: Black Feminism and the Cult of Masculinity: The Danger Within," *The Black Scholar, 10,* 63-67.

652. Staples, Robert (1980). "Racial and Cultural Variations Among American Families: A Decennial Review of the Literature on Minority Families," *Journal of Marriage and the Family, 42,* 887-903.

653. Staples, Robert (1981, May/June). "Black Manhood in the 1970s: A Critical Look Back," *The Black Scholar,* 2-9.

654. Staples, Robert (1985). "Changes in Black Family Structure: The Conflict Between Family Ideology and Structural Conditions," *Journal of Marriage and the Family, 47,* 1005-1013.

655. Staples, Robert (1986). "The Political Economy of Black Family Life," *The Black Scholar, 17,* 2-11.

656. Staples, Robert (1987). "Black Male Genocide: A Final Solution to the Race Problem in America," *The Black Scholar, 18,* 2-11.

657. Staples, Robert (1987). "Social Structure and Black Family Life: An Analysis of Current Trends," *Journal of Black Studies, 17,* 267-86.

658. Staples, Robert (1991). "Social Inequality and Black Sexual Pathology: The Essential Relationship," *The Black Scholar, 21*(3), 29-37.

659. Starr, J. (1994, Summer). "The Resurrection of Black Martyrs," in *Berkeley McNair Journal*, v2, http://www-mcnair.berkeley.edu/uga/ost/ mcnair/.

660. Stephens, Brooke M. (ed.). *Men We Cherish: African American Women Praise the Men in Their Lives*. New York: Doubleday, 1997.

661. Stewart, J. and Scott, J. (1978). "The Institutional Decimation of Black American Males," *Western Journal of Black Studies, 2*, 82-93.

662. Stewart, J.B. and Hyclak, T.J. (1986). "The Effects of Immigrants, Women, and Teenagers on the Relative Earnings of Black Males," *The Review of Black Political Economy, 15*, 93-101.

663. Stewart, Ron. *African-American Husbands: A Study of Black Family Life*. Bristol, IN: Wyndham Hall Press, 1991.

664. Stroman, C.A. (1989). "To Be Young, Male, and Black on Prime-time Television," *Urban Research Review, 12*(1), 9-10.

665. Sudarkasa, N. (1992). "Don't Write Off Thomas," *The Black Scholar, 22*(1-2), 99-100.

666. Taylor, Clarence. *Knocking at Our Own Door: Milton A. Galamison and the Struggle to Integrate New York City Schools*. New York: Columbia University Press, 1997.

667. Taylor, R.J., Leashore, B.R. and Toliver, S. (1988). "An Assessment of the Provider Role as Perceived by Black Males," *Family Relations, 27*, 426-31.

668. Taylor, R.L. (1981). "Psychological Modes of Adaptation," in Gary, Lawrence E. (ed.), *Black Men*. Beverly Hills, CA: Sage Publications.

669. Terry, Roderick (compiler). *Brother's Keeper: Words of Inspiration for African-American Men*. White Plains, NY: Peter Pauper Press, 1996.

670. Thomas, C.W. (1987). "Pride and Purpose as Antidotes to Black Homicidal Violence," *Journal of the National Medical Association, 79*(2), 155-160.

671. Thompson, E.H. and Pleck, J. (1987). "The Structure of Male Role Norms," in Kimmel, M. (ed.), *Changing Men, New Directions in*

Research on Men and Masculinity. Newbury Park, CA: Sage Publications.

672. Tinney, J.S. (1981). "The Religious Experience of Black Men," in Gary, L.E. (Ed.), *Black Men*. Beverly Hills, CA: Sage Publications.

673. Toldson, I.L. and Pasteur, A.B. (1993). "The Black Male Mystique: At Once Admired and Feared. An Exposition of What it Means to be Black and Male in America," *Journal of African-American Male Studies, 1*(2), 70-77.

674. Tuck, S. (1971). "A Model for Working With Black Fathers," *American Journal of Orthopsychiatry, 38,* 715-723.

675. Tucker, D.M. *Black Pastors and Leaders: Memphis, 1819-1972*. Memphis, TN: Memphis State University Press, 1975.

676. Tucker, M.B. (1987). "The Black Male Shortage in Los Angeles," *Sociology and Social Research, 71*(3), 221-231.

677. Turner, D.T. (1995). "Visions of Love and Manliness in a Blackening World: Dramas and Black Life Since 1953," *The Black Scholar, 25*(2), 2-12.

678. Urban Institute (1995). "Nurturing Young Black Males: Programs that Work," Urban Institute Publications, Washington, DC.

679. Vanzant, Iyanla. *The Spirit of a Man: A Vision of Transformation for Black Men and the Women Who Love Them*. San Francisco: Harper, 1996.

680. Vontress, Clemmont (1971). "The Black Male Personality," *The Black Scholar, 2*(10), 10-17.

681. Vontress, Clemmont (1971). "A Response to Robert Staples," *The Black Scholar, 3*(3), 46-49.

682. Walters, Ronald W. *Black Presidential Politics in America: A Strategic Approach*. Albany, NY: State University of New York Press, 1988.

683. Washington, Elsie B. *Uncivil War: The Struggle Between Black Men and Women*. Chicago, IL: Noble Press, 1996.

684. *Washington Post* (1991, April 5). "Recalling the Legend of Lee Atwater," pg. B1, B2.

685. Watkins, C.A. (1971). "Simple: The Alter Ego of Langston Hughes," *The Black Scholar, 2*(10), 18-26.

686. Watson, Clifford. *Ten Great African-American Men of Science: With Hands-On Science Activities.* Maywood, NJ: Peoples Publishing Group, 1995.

687. Watts, Roderick J. and Jagers, Robert J. (eds.). *Manhood Development in Urban African-American Communities.* New York: Haworth Press, 1997.

688. Weatherspoon, Floyd D. *African-American Males and the Law: Cases and Material.* Lanham, MD: University Press of America, 1998.

689. Wheelan, B.S. (1991) "Making Public Education Work for Black Males," paper presented at the National Conference on Preventing and Treating Alcohol and Other Drug Abuse, HIV Infection, and AIDS in the Black Community.

690. Wiggins, W.H. (1971). "Jack Johnson as Bad Nigger: The Folklore of His Life," *The Black Scholar, 2*(5), 35-46.

691. Wilkinson, D. (1977). "The Stigmatization Process of the Black Male's Identity," in Wilkinson, D. and Taylor, R. (eds.), *The Black Male in America.* Chicago: Nelson-Hall.

692. Williams, Armstrong. *Beyond Blame: How We Can Succeed by Breaking the Dependency Barrier.* New York: Free Press, 1995.

693. Williams, Armstrong. *Letters to a Young Victim: Hope and Healing in America's Inner Cities.* New York: Free Press, 1996.

694. Wilmore, G. (ed.). *Black Men in Prison: The Response of the African-American Church.* Vol. 2 in the *Black Church Scholars Series.* Atlanta, GA: The ITC Press, 1990.

695. Wilson, A.N. *Understanding Black Adolescent Male Violence: Its Remediation and Prevention.* New York: Afrikan World Infosystems, 1992.

696. Wilson, C.E., Jr. (1993). "Myths and Confusions in *Straight Out of Brooklyn* and *Boyz N the Hood*," *Journal of African-American Male Studies, 1*(2), 78-86.

697. Wilson-Brewer, R. and Jacklin, B. (1990). "Violence Prevention Strategies Targeted at the General Population of Minority Youth," background paper presented for the Forum on Youth Violence in Minority Communities: Setting the Agenda for Prevention, sponsored by the Educational Development Center, Inc., Atlanta, GA.

698. Woodson, Carter G. (1933). "The New Type of Professional Man Required," in *The Miseducation of the Negro*. Washington, DC: Associated Publishers.

699. X, Malcolm. *By Any Means Necessary: Speeches, Interviews, and a Letter by Malcolm X*. New York: Pathfinder, 1970.

700. Young, V.H. (1970). "Family and Childhood in a Southern Negro Community," *American Anthropologist, 120*, 269-288.

16

Dissertations

701. Abernethy, A.D. (1986). "Hypertension, Stress, and Affect: A Study of Anger." University of California, Berkeley.

702. Adams, M.L. (1990). "Improving the Potential for Success of Inner-City Black Male Youths: A Case Study of the Fifth Ward Enrichment Program." University of Texas at Austin.

703. Arnold, H.E. (1986). "Discrimination or Disintegration: Factors Affecting the Relative Earnings Position of Black Males During the 1960's and 1970's." Florida State University.

704. Barnes, R.W. (1987). "High School Completion, Self-Concept and Psychopathology among Black Male Drug Abusers." Howard University.

705. Barnett, R. (1991). "Planning, Developing, and Designing a Role Model Educational Program for African-American Students." Fordham University.

706. Bell, D.M. (1994). "Giving Voice to Black Male Students and Black Male Secondary Educators: An Exploration into the Black American Male Teacher Shortage." University of Maryland College Park.

707. Benedict, W.R. (1994).   "Return to the Scene of the Punishment: Recidivism of Adult Male Felons on Probation, 1986, 1989." Kansas State University.

708. Bishop, T.F. (1994). "A Christian Africentric Model for the Initiation of African-American Males into Manhood." United Theological Seminary.

709. Black, D.P. (1993). "The Black Male Concept of Manhood as Portrayed in Selected Slave and Free Narratives (1794-1863)." Temple University.

710. Blumenthal, J.M. (1994). "Do You Hear Me Though? Voices of Young Black Males in Arizona's Juvenile Corrections System." Arizona State University.

711. Bobino, R.F. (1986). "African-American Fathers and Daughters: The Adult Developmental Consequences of the Retreat of Fathers During their Daughters' Adolescence." Wright Institute.

712. Bolster, W.J. (1992). "African-American Seamen: Race, Seafaring Work, and Atlantic Maritime Culture, 1750-1860." Johns Hopkins University.

713. Bosman, S.C.M. (1985). "The Utilization of the Bender-Gestalt Test with Black Men" (Afrikaans Text). University of Pretoria (South Africa).

714. Botkin, S.D. (1988).   "Male Gender Consciousness: A Study of Undergraduate College Men." University of Massachusetts.

715. Boxley, R.L. (1973).   "Sex-Object Choice in Adult Black Males: Perception of Parental Relationships and Early Sexual Behavior." University of Washington.

716. Braden, W.R. (1993).   "Homies: a Study of Peer-Mentoring among African-American Males in Chicago in Relation to Adult Education." Northern Illinois University.

717. Brice, B.E.G. (1992). "A Study of Persistence of Freshman Males at Two Historically Black Institutions of Higher Education." Georgia State University.

718. Broome, L.J. (1990). "Sex, Violence, and History: Images of Black Men in the Selected Fiction of Gayle Jones, Alice Walker, and Toni Morrison." Bowling Green State University.

719. Brown, C.M. (1993). "Stagolee: from Shack Bully to Culture Hero." University of California, Berkeley.

720. Brown-Cheatham, M.A. (1990). "An Assessment of Object-Relations and Self-Concept in Black Father-Absent Male Children as a Consequence of the Father's Control of His Absence." City University of New York.

721. Bryan, D.G. (1991). "Unheard Echoes in the Education of Black Males." Syracuse University.

722. Buchanan, S.C. (1987). "A Critical Analysis of Style in Four Black Jubilee Quartets in the United States." New York University.

723. Bufford, R.E. (1984). "The Relationship of Socio-Economic Status to Self-Disclosure among Black Male High School Students." New York University.

724. Burrell, W.A. (1988). "Selected Correlates of Successful Occupational Attainment among Black Men and Women." Howard University.

725. Burroughs, J.A. (1991). "Study of the Pragmatic Language Skills of Lower Socio-Economic Black Male Preschoolers." University of Oklahoma Health Sciences Center.

726. Burtless, G.T. (1977) "Taxes, Transfers, and Preferences for Work among Married Black Men: The Gary Income Maintenance Experiment." Massachusetts Institute of Technology.

727. Butner, B. (1978). "Effects of Prestige, Peer, Teacher and Alternate Culture Teacher Modeling on Measures of Honesty Behavior of Fifth & Sixth Grade Black Males." Catholic University of America.

728. Byun, Y. (1991). "Compositional and Processual Aspects of Living Arrangements among Elderly Black Men and White Men with European Heritage Across Developmental Time." Utah State University.

729. Caldwell, C.H. (1986). "Motivation and Patterns of Medical Services Utilization among Black Male Veterans and Non-Veterans." University of Michigan.

730. Calhoun, F.S. (1977). "Child-Rearing Practices of the Black Father." California State University, Long Beach.

731. Campbell, D.B. (1996). "The Fear of Success and its Relationship to Racial Identity Attitudes and Achievement Behavior among Black Male College Students." City University of New York.

732. Campbell, K.E. (1993). "The Rhetoric of Black English Vernacular: A Study of the Oral and Written Discourse Practices of African-American Male College Students." Ohio State University.

733. Carey, S.A. (1992). "Black Men's du Boisian Relationships to Southern Social Institutions in the Novels of John Oliver Killens." University of Texas at Dallas.

734. Carter, S.D. (1982). "The Self-Esteem and Job Satisfaction of Black Male Professional Level College Graduates as Related to the Racial Identity of College Attended." Rutgers The State University of New Jersey, New Brunswick.

735. Causey, V. (1993). "Factors Related to Academic Performance of Black, Urban, Male, Middle School Students from One-Parent Homes." Washington State University.

736. Cazenave, N.A. (1977). "Middle-Income Black Fathers: Family Interaction, Transaction, and Development." Tulane University.

737. Chaplin, D.D. (1993). "Employment Bust or Education Boom? Black Teenage Males: 1960-1988." University of Wisconsin, Madison.

738. Chapman, I.T. (1991). "A Qualitative Analysis of Selected Black Male Students Interfacing with Writing Literacy." University of South Carolina.

739. Chay, K.Y. (1996). "An Empirical Analysis of Black Economic Progress over Time." Princeton University.

740. Chepp, T.J. (1975). "The Relationship of Cognitive Style to the Attainment of Success among Selected Disadvantaged, Young Adult, Black Males." Catholic University of America.

741. Claassen, M. (1994). "The African Profile Technique: A Diagnostic Aid for Black Male Psychiatric Patients" (Afrikaans Text). University of Pretoria (South Africa).

742. Clark, K.S. (1993). "Reforming the Black Male Self: A Study of Subject Formation in Selected Works by James Baldwin, Ernest Gaines, and August Wilson." University of North Carolina at Chapel Hill.

743. Coleman, P.P. (1981). "Separation and Autonomy: Issues of Adolescent Identity Development among the Families of Black Male Status Offenders." Wright Institute.

744. Cook, V.S. (1971). "A Comparison of Work Values of Disadvantaged Black Males with Work Values of Advantaged Males in an Urban Setting." Catholic University of America.

745. Cooke, A.L. (1974). "A Comparison of Middle-Class College-Educated Black Men in Traditional and Nontraditional Occupations." Ohio State University.

746. Costner, B.K. (1989). "Black Male Public Administrators: Training and Upward Mobility." Kentucky State University.

747. Cotten, J.F.H. (1995). "Distal Fatherhood: a Study of Black Fathers Who Live Away From Their Children." University of Texas at Austin.

748. Coward-Reid, M.F. (1995). "A Case Study of the Concerned Black Men of Richmond Mentor Program for African-American Males: Program Structure and Practices, Perceptions of Strengths and Weaknesses, Mentor-Protege Relationships." Virginia Polytechnic Institute and State University.

749. Craig, J.M., Sr. (1990). "The Effects of Academic Games on the Attitude Toward School of Third-Grade Black Males." University of Southern Mississippi.

750. Crane, V. (1972). "Effects of Black or White Adult Modeling With or Without Rule Structure on Adopting A Standard for Self-Control in Six- to Eleven-year Old Black Boys." Fordham University.

751. Cropp, D.E.B. (1996). "Family and Societal Processes Affecting Achievement in African-American College Men: An Ethnographic Multiple Case Study." Miami University.

752. Cubie, M.V. (1988). "The Missing Link in the Afrocentric Model: Employment and the Role of the Black Father." Wright Institute.

753. Dance, L.J. (1995). "Streetwise Versus Schoolwise: The Attitudes of Urban and Inner City Youth Towards School." Harvard University.

754. Daniel, J.E. (1975). "A Definition of Fatherhood as Expressed by Black Fathers." University of Pittsburgh.

755. Davis, A.C. (1984). "Cardiovascular Reactivity, Anger Management and Personality Traits among Young Black Males." University of Southern California.

756. Davis, C., Jr. (1993). "The Alpha-Omega Young Men's Association of H. D. Woodson Senior High School as an Alternative to Parental, Adult, And Community Involvement in Urban Black Males." University of Massachusetts.

757. Davis, C.E., Jr. (1983). "Child Rearing Patterns and Job Satisfaction of Fathers With Behavior Disorder Boys." University of North Carolina at Chapel Hill.

758. Davis, M.A. (1990). "Problems (Encounters) Black High School Seniors Face Preparing for College." Columbia University Teachers College

759. Davis, S., Jr. (1972). "A Study of the High School Success Patterns of a Group of Black Males through High School." Wayne State University.

760. Dillard, J.M. (1976). "A Correlational Study of Middle-Class Black Males' Vocational Maturity and Self-Concept." State University of New York at Buffalo.

761. Dowdell, J.B. (1996). "The Dilemma of Dealing with the Black Male Dropout Problem." University of Pennsylvania.

762. Dudley, T.V.J. (1993). "An Analysis of Selected Black Male Achievers and Non-Achievers of the 1992 Graduating Class of Jones High School, Orlando, Florida." University of Central Florida.

763. Dunlap, E.E. (1988). "Male-Female Relations and the Black Family." University of California, Berkeley.

764. Edwards, A.W. (1990). "Increasing Health Care Awareness in Black Males with Essential Hypertension." Wright Institute.

765. Edwards, G.W. (1987). "An Analysis of the Image of the Black Male in Major Novels By White Writers from 1852 to 1971." Harvard University.

766. Ellis, M.L. (1992). "'Rain down Fire': The Lynching of Sam Hose." Florida State University.

767. Erbe, B.M. (1973). "The Redistribution of Black Males in American Occupational Structure: 1950-1970." University of Iowa.

768. Farr, J.B. (1982). "Black Odyssey: The Seafaring Traditions of Afro-Americans." University of California, Santa Barbara.

769. Faulkner, R. (1989). "Criteria for Counselor Selection among Black Male College Students: An Opinion Survey." Tennessee State University.

770. Ferguson, A.A. (1995). "Bad Boys: School and the Social Construction of Black Masculinity." University of California, Berkeley.

771. Ferguson, S.E. (1990). "The Effects of the Getting Away Clean Program on Disruptive School Behaviors in the Black Male Child." Virginia Polytechnic Institute and State University.

772. Finley, R. (1992). "The Freedmen's Bureau in Arkansas." University of Arkansas.

773. Flagg, A. (1985). "Factors Influencing College Choice of Black Males in Middle Tennessee." Kent State University.

774. Fleming, G.J. (1995). "The College Attendance Plans of Male High School Students And Their Perception of the Quality of Education Received." University of South Carolina.

775. Fossett, M.A. (1983). "Racial Income Inequality and Market Discrimination in Metropolitan Areas of the United States in 1970." University of Texas at Austin.

776. Foy, C.T. (1985). "Achievement of Elementary School Children in Father Absent Homes." Columbia University Teachers College.

777. Francois, T.V. (1977). "The Engagement of Adolescent Black Males in Psychotherapy: The Relation of Role Induction, Locus-of-Control and Depression." New York University.

778. Friedberg, P.M. (1993). "Reading to Read: Effects of Increasing Oral Reading Fluency on the Non-Targeted Skill of Reading Comprehension." University of Southern Mississippi.

779. Fuller, W. (1982). "The Definition, Etiology and Treatment of Mental Illness among Adult Black Males with Middle and Low Socioeconomic Backgrounds." University of Northern Colorado.

780. Galbraith, C.S.B. (1984). "The Relationship of Auditory Sequential Memory Tasks and Deficits in Reading Performed by Black Males in Grades 2, 3, and 4." Temple University.

781. Gary-Williams, G.E. (1986). "Wellbeing of Retired Black Males Measured by Selected Psychosocial Variables." University of Maryland College Park.

782. Gelber, S.M. (1972). "Black Men and Businessmen: Business Attitudes Toward Negro Employment, 1945-1967." University of Wisconsin, Madison.

783. George, L. (1985). "Assaultive Behavior of Hospitalized Schizophrenics." City University of New York.

784. Gibbs, J.M. (1985). "Causative Factors Related to Criminal Involvement among Young, Low Income, Black Males." Boston College.

785. Gibson, J.O. (1991). "A Comparison of the Attitudes of Selected Adolescents Regarding Moral Norms and Social Conventions." University of Illinois at Chicago.

786. Givens, E., III (1988). "Black Family Structure: Perceived Support for Mental Health and Chemically Dependent Clients." Boston University.

787. Goggin, D.J. (1994). "Situational vs. Structural Causes of Homelessness among Single Black Men in Orange County, California." California State University, Long Beach.

788. Gooden, W.E. (1980). "The Adult Development of Black Men." (Volumes I and II). Yale University.

789. Goodwin, A.S. (1989). "A Content Analysis of the Portrayal of Black Male Adolescent Protagonists in Four Novels for Adolescents

(Armstrong, Lipsyte, Parks, Bonham)." University of Maryland College Park.

790. Grant, N.L., Jr. (1995). "Jean Toomer and Zora Neale Hurston: Modernism and the Recovery of the Black Male Identity." New York University.

791. Gray, A.R. (1994). "The African-American Male's Family Relationships in Black Plays: Their Evolution and Meaning." City University of New York.

792. Green, J., III (1975). "A Comparison of Culturally-Congruent TAT Stimuli among Black Males." Stephen F. Austin State University.

793. Green, J.W. (1991). "An Investigation of the Impact of Locus-Of-Control, Expectancy of Success and Family Involvement on the Academic Success of Young Black Males." Wayne State University.

794. Green, M.E.P. (1988). "Peer Coaction Effects on Delay of Gratification Behavior among Black Preschool Boys." Columbia University.

795. Green, Z. (1989). "Black Youth, Academic Achievement, Mentoring, Alienation, And Self-Efficacy." Boston University.

796. Groce, J.T., Sr. (1988). "Perceived Factors in the Early Lives of Black Males That Have Influenced Their Later Life Development." Temple University.

797. Hamid, R. (1976). "The Modification of Compliant Behavior of Black Males in Biracial Settings." Saint Louis University.

798. Harris, E.W. (1995). "Identification and Analysis of Significant Factors That Influence Black Male High School Students to Take College-Preparatory Mathematics Classes." Harvard University.

799. Hawkeswood, W.G. (1991). "'One of the Children': An Ethnography of Identity and Gay Black Men." Columbia University.

800. Heffernon, A.W.(1969). "The Effect of Race and Assumed Professional Status of Male Lay Counselors Upon Eighth Grade Black Males' Perceptions of and Reactions to the Counseling Process." University of California, Berkeley.

801. Henderson, E.I. (1990). "Whites' Avoidance of Blacks as a Function of Observing a Negative Interaction with a Black." University of Michigan.

802. Herbert, J.I. (1985). "Adult Psychosocial Development: The Evolution of the Individual Life Structure of Black Male Entrepreneurs." Yale University.

803. Herrington, E. (1989). "The Experience of the Black Male Adolescent in Psychotherapy." California Institute of Integral Studies.

804. Hines, B.J.L. (1989). "The Relationship Between Nurturance, Parenting Attitudes and Behaviors, and Marital Adjustment in Black Fathers." University of Tennessee.

805. Hodes, M.E. (1991). "Sex Across the Color Line: White Women and Black Men in the Nineteenth Century American South." Princeton University.

806. Hopson, C.L. (1993). "A Psychological Portrait of the African-American Male Student in the Public Schools." University of Oregon.

807. Hughes, M.J. (1995). "Breaking the Cycle of Destructive Behaviors: Facilitating Positive Developmental Change in African and Latino-American Males, 18-28." Brandeis University, F. Heller Graduate School For Advanced Studies in Social Welfare.

808. Jackson, J., Sr. (1993). "A Comparative Study of High and Low Achieving Inner-City African-American Sophomore Males' Expectations of Self, In-School and Out-Of-School Support." Western Michigan University.

809. Jackson, M.S. (1988). "Drug Use and Delinquency in the Black Male Adolescent: A Descriptive Study." Case Western Reserve University.

810. James-Brown, F.L. (1995). "The Black Male Crisis in the Classroom: a Qualitative Study of the Educational Experiences of Black Male Students as Perceived by the Students Themselves, Their Teachers, and Parents." Ohio State University.

811. James, C.B. (1982). "Primitives on the Move: Some Historical Articulations of Garvey and Garveyism, 1887-1927." University of California, Los Angeles.

812. Jenkins, M. (1994). "Fear of the 'Gangsta': Policy Responses to Gang Activity In the City of Boston (Massachusetts)." Northeastern University.

813. Johnson, E.L. (1979). "Mate Selection: Preferences of Black Single College Males With Reference to Selected Variables." Indiana State University.

814. Johnson, E.M. (1988). "Predictors of Drug Abuse among a Group of Urban Black Male Adolescents." University of Maryland at Baltimore.

815. Johnson, P.D. (1996). "Beyond the Timberline: The Stories of Five Black Males at A Predominately White University." New York University.

816. Johnson, W.E. (1992). "An Investigation of a Select Group of Black Fifth-Grade Male Students' Perceptions of Their Self-Concepts." Clark Atlanta University.

817. Jones, B.A. (1994). "Effects of a Mentor Program on the Academic Success and Self Concept of Selected Black Males in the Junior High School." Virginia Polytechnic Institute and State University.

818. Jones, E.L. (1987). "The Relation of Object Relations and Selected Personality Characteristics to Sexual Object Preferences of Adult Black Males." New York University.

819. Jones, R.M. (1995). "A Comparative Analysis of the Effect of Race on the Discipline Judgments of Biracial, Black, and White Male Children." California School of Professional Psychology, San Diego.

820. Jones, S.E. (1996). "Disconnected Connection: The Road to Being a Black Man." University of Maryland College Park.

821. Joseph, H.M., Jr. (1982). "Black Fathers and Their Sons: The Impact of a Modeling Intervention." Boston University Graduate School.

822. Katzenstein, H. (1972). "Private and Social Benefits of the College Degree for Black Males 1962-1970: A Sample Study of Graduates of the City College of New York and Howard University." City University of New York.

823. Kim, T. (1995). "Place or Person?: A Labor Market Analysis of Central City Poverty." Carnegie-Mellon University.

824. King, L.M. (1972). "An Experimental Exploration of the Relationship Between Self-Reinforcement, Self-Esteem and Locus-of-Control in 9-11 Year Old Black Males." University of California, Los Angeles.

825. Kirk, A.R. (1976). "Socio-Psychological Factors in Attempted Suicide among Urban Black Males." Michigan State University.

826. Kliman, A.J. (1988). "Rising Joblessness among Black Male Youth, 1950-1980: A Regional Analysis." University of Utah.

827. Krogh, M.C. (1995). "The Chicago Economy and the Employment of Black Men in the Inner City, 1969-1987." University of Chicago.

828. Labrecque, S.V. (1976). "Child-Rearing Attitudes and Observed Behaviors of Black Fathers with Kindergarten Daughters." Florida State University.

829. Lanier, A.K. (1991). "Black Male Adolescents: The Effects of Ethnicity and Perceived Performance on Academic Performance and Self-Confidence." University of Denver.

830. Larson, T.E. (1986). "Job Placement of Young Black Males: The Roles of Migration and Structural Change in Urban Labor Markets." University of California, Berkeley.

831. Laseter, R.L. (1994). "Young Inner-City African-American Men: Work and Family Life." University of Chicago.

832. Lattimore, V.L., III (1984). "Pastoral Care Strategies of Black Pastors." Northwestern University.

833. Lemelle, A.J. (1984). "Racial Oppression and School Delinquency: A Reconsideration of Deviance Theories." University of California, Berkeley.

834. Lesnett, F.S. (1975). "Exploratory Review of the Effects of Various Sociological Variables and a Negative Income Tax on the Changes in Labor Supply of Urban Black Males." Purdue University.

835. Lewis, G.F. (1982). "An Analysis of Interviews with Urban Black Males who Dropped out of High School (Pennsylvania)." Temple University.

836. Lockman, P.T., Jr. (1984). "Black Male Employment as a Social Bond to Society." University of Colorado at Boulder.

837. Long, R.M. (1985). "A Case Study: Five Illiterate Black Men in a Literate Society." George Washington University.

838. Madison, P.L. (1987). "Effects of Unemployment on the Black Married Males' Self-Esteem and Family Relations." University of Pittsburgh.

839. Majors, R.G., III (1987). "Cool Pose: A New Approach Toward a Systematic Understanding and Study of Black Male Behavior." University of Illinois at Urbana-Champaign.

840. Mallon, W.T. (1996). "Voicing Manhood: Masculinity and Dialogue in Ernest J. Gaines's 'The Sky in Gray,' 'Three Men,' and 'Gathering of Old Men.'" University of Richmond.

841. Marshall, B.N. (1992). "The High School Teacher/Mentor Program: A Descriptive Study of its Impact on Career Choices. African-American Male Participants." University of Louisville.

842. Martin, B.E. (1992). "Interpersonal Helplessness and the Wish for Nurturance among Conduct Disordered Black Male Adolescents." City University of New York

843. Mason, S.D. (1976). "The Effects of Peer-Resolution Skills Training on a Group of Black Boys Living in a High Crime Area." Atlanta University.

844. McCullough, Y.P. (1995). "Motivators for Success: Personal and Familial Drives among Adolescent Black Males." Barry University School of Social Work.

845. Melton, W., III (1977). "Self-Satisfaction and Martial Stability among Black Males: Socioeconomic and Demographic Antecedents." Washington State University.

846. Mohamed, R.A. (1980). "Race, Sex and Therapist's Perceived Competence." University of Southern California.

847. Moisan, P.A. (1994). "Psychological Outcome of Sexually Abused Black and Latino Boys." California School of Professional Psychology, Los Angeles.

848. Moore, P.L. (1996). "W.E.B. DuBois: A Critical Study of His Philosophy of Education and its Relevance for Three Contemporary Issues in Education of Significance to African-Americans." Wayne State University.

849. Moore, P.R. (1991). "Career and Marriage among Professional Black Couples." Texas Tech University.

850. Moore-Pollock, S. (1990). "A Comparison of Black and White Male Alcoholics on Alcoholism-Treatment Outcome." University of Missouri, Kansas City.

851. Moore, S.E. (1992). "A Comparative Analysis of Adolescent Chemical Dependency Treatment Programs in Allegheny County, Pennsylvania with A Special Focus on the Black Male Adolescent Who Uses Heroin and/or Crack/Cocaine." University of Pittsburgh.

852. Muckley, P.A. (1992). "Black American Author-Biography: From Politics to Myth and Beyond." Temple University.

853. Murray, M.M. (1982). "The Middle Years of Life of Middle Class Black Men: An Exploratory Study." University of Cincinnati.

854. Myers, O.L. (1996). "Effects of Interscholastic Athletic Involvement on the Personal Development of Black Male High School Students." Virginia Polytechnic Institute and State University.

855. Nall, H.A. (1982). "Just like Brothers: An Ethnographic Approach to the Friendship Ties of an Urban Group of Elderly Black Men." University of California, Los Angeles.

856. Neal, A.A. (1988). "Religious Involvement and Practices Concerning the Use of Alcohol among Black Adolescents." University of South Carolina.

857. Neverdon-Merritt, M. (1996). "The Socialization of the Urban, Black, Male Delinquent in A Low-Income, Single-Parent, Female-Headed Household." University of Maryland at Baltimore.

858. Njoku, R.E.(1995). "Toward a Comprehensive Explanation of the Black Urban Underclass Phenomenon: Theory, Empirical Evidence, and Public Policy." University of Akron.

859. Nordmoe, D.I. (1992). "Social Pathology among Urban Black Males: An Explanatory Model for Variation in Mortality Rates Across Metropolitan Statistical Areas." Wayne State University.

860. Nubukpo, K.M. (1987). "Through Their Sisters' Eyes: The Representation of Black Men in the Novels of Toni Morrison, Alice Walker, and Toni Cade Bambara." Boston University.

861. Oby, J.B. (1996). "Equity in Operatic Casting as Perceived by African-American Male Singers." Florida State University

862. Ochs, S.J. (1985). "Deferred Mission: The Josephites and the Struggle for Black Catholic Priests, 1871-1960 (Volumes I, II, and III) (St. Joseph's Society, John R. Slattery)." University of Maryland College Park.

863. Oliver, W. (1993). "Violent Confrontations Between Black Males in Bars and Bar Settings." State University of New York at Albany.

864. Orange, C.M. (1991). "Motivation and Vicarious Empowerment of Black Male Adolescents Through Simulation and Structured Experiences." Washington University.

865. Oshodi, J.E. (1991). "Achievement Motivation in Native and Immigrant Blacks." Miami Institute of Psychology of the Caribbean Center for Advanced Studies.

866. Parmer, T. (1987). "A Descriptive Study of the Career Dreams, Career Decisiveness and Career Choice of Urban Black Male and Female Athlete and Nonathlete High School Students." University of Iowa.

867. Parson, N.M. (1989). "Factors Related to the Incarceration and Non-Incarceration Of Black Men Raised in Christian Churches." University of Nevada, Reno.

868. Paschall, M.J. (1995). "Determinants of Violent Behavior by Black Male Adolescents: A Panel Study." University of North Carolina at Chapel Hill.

869. Pate, A.P., Jr. (1992). "An Ethnographic Inquiry into the Relationship Between Selected Cultural Factors and High Achievement of Three Black Male Primary School Students from Single-Parent Homes Situated in a

Low-Income Federally Funded Housing Project: A Multiple Case Study."
Miami University.

870. Peacock, R. (1990). "The Black Male Streetchild: An Explorative
Psychocriminological Study (Afrikaans Text)." University of Pretoria
(South Africa).

871. Pendleton, O.H., Jr. (1995). "Follow-Up Study of Black Male Basketball
Players Who Did Not Graduate from Selected Atlantic Coast Division I
Institutions." George Washington University.

872. Pennington, G. (1984). "Inhibited Power Motivation, Locus of Control,
Active Coping Style, and Blood Pressure Differences among Black Male
Adolescents." University of North Carolina at Chapel Hill.

873. Phillips, C.O. (1981). "Assessing Black Male High School Students'
Attitudes Toward Vocational Education." Southern Illinois University at
Carbondale.

874. Pickron, C. (1991). "The Experience of Black Male Administrators at
Predominantly White Four-Year Institutions of Higher Education."
University of Massachusetts.

875. Plass, M.S. (1990). "Homicide in Black Families: A Quantitative
Analysis of Trends and Patterns in the United States." University of New
Hampshire.

876. Pokross, W.R. (1977) "The Occupational Participation of Younger Black
Men: Variation Among and Recent Changes in the Larger Metropolitan
Areas." University of Pittsburgh.

877. Pullman, W.E. (1994). "Serving the Needs of at Risk Youth: Community
Based Programs for Young Black Men." Virginia Commonwealth
University.

878. Raeardon, E.M. (1994). "The Structure of Demand and Black Relative
Economic Progress, 1940-1990." University of Chicago.

879. Ransom, E. (1995). "Developing a Mentorship Program Model for Black
Males as a Prison Ministry in an Urban Congregation." Wesley
Theological Seminary.

880. Ratcliff, K.S. (1977). "In Their Thirties: A Study of the Young Adult Outcomes in a Sample of Urban Black Males." University of Wisconsin, Madison.

881. Ray, A.A. (1994). "Disciplinary Problems as a Function of Satisfaction: A Study of Black Male High School Students." State University of New York at Buffalo.

882. Rise, E.W. (1992). "The Martinsville Seven and Southern Justice: Race, Crime, And Capital Punishment in Virginia, 1949-1951." University of Florida.

883. Rivers, R.M. (1995). "Adult Black Males' Perceptions of Factors Associated with Their Perception in Risky Health Behaviors as Adolescents." University of Florida.

884. Roberson, B. (1993). "Winning and Losing Black Male Track Coaches: a Personality-Traits Profile." United States International University.

885. Roberts, H.B. (1983). "Psychological World of the Black Juvenile Delinquent: Three Case Studies." New Brunswick, State University of New Jersey.

886. Rock, J.L. (1995). "Tipping the Scales: Access to an Academic Curriculum as a Factor in Explaining the Wage Differential between Black and White Men in the 1980s." Harvard University.

887. Rodgers, W.M., III (1993). "Employment and Earnings of Young Males: 1979-1991." Harvard University.

888. Rolison, G.L. (1987). The Political Economy of the Urban Underclass: Black Subemployment in Advanced Capitalism. University of California, Santa Cruz.

889. Ronde, S.B.B. (1985). "Ten Black Men Who 'Made It': Contributions of Victors Over Circumstance to a Theory of Development." Columbia University.

890. Rose, D. (1989). "Mortality in Black and White Connecticut Males, by Socioeconomic Status, 1960-1980." Yale University.

891. Ross, M. (1993). "Building Positive Images in African-American Males through the Sunday School from a Black Perspective." United Theological Seminary.

892. Ross, W., Jr. (1987). "A Descriptive Study of the Characteristics of the Home Environments of High-Achieving and Low-Achieving Fourth-Grade Black Male Students in a Small Rural Community." University of South Carolina.

893. Sams, C. (1994). "Developing and Implementing a Church Based Tutorial Program." Drew University.

894. Samuels, H.P. (1991). "The Relationship among Socioeconomic Status, Religiosity, Attitudes Toward Sexuality and Sexual Experience in Black and White Heterosexual Males." New York University.

895. Schuster, F.A. (1979). "An Analysis of the Effects that Attitude Toward Work and Job Satisfaction Have on the Performance of Black Males Employed as CETA Custodial Workers." Northern Illinois University.

896. Schutte, J.E. (1979). "Growth and Body Composition of Lower and Middle Income Adolescent Black Males." Southern Methodist University.

897. Scott, E.E. (1984). "An Analysis of the Sociological Portrayal of the Black American Male's Inclusion in the California State-Adopted Reading Series." University of San Francisco.

898. Seaberry, J.S. (1994). "Familial and Environmental Factors Shaping the Experiences of a Black Male Collegian: A Qualitative Inquiry." University of Nebraska, Lincoln.

899. Seymour, D.P. (1994). "An Exploration of Corporate Career Advancement: the African-American Male in New York Money Center Banks." Walden University.

900. Sheffey, M.A. (1982). "Holland's Theory: Concurrent Validity for College Educated Black Males." University of Florida.

901. Shirvanian, H. (1983). "Factors Affecting the Level of Black Male Industrial Workers' Job Satisfaction." United States International University.

902. Smith, E.H. (1995). "Interpretation of Meanings in Classroom Interactions: Three Teachers and Their African-American Male Students." University of Arizona.

903. Smith, L.A. (1989). "Windows on Opportunities: An Exploration in Program Development for Black Adolescent Fathers." City University of New York.

904. Smith, L.D. (1982). "The Drinking Practices of Black Physicians." University of Pittsburgh.

905. Smith, R.L. (1994). "Effect of Black Manhood Training on Adolescent African-American Males." Temple University.

906. Sommerville, D.M. (1995). "The Rape Myth Reconsidered: The Intersection of Race, Class and Gender in the American South, 1800-1877." Rutgers, the State University of New Jersey, New Brunswick.

907. Spence, C.M. (1996). "The Effects of Sport Participation on the Academic and Career Aspirations of Black Male Student Athletes in Toronto High Schools." University of Toronto (Canada).

908. Spurlock, G.P., III (1994). "Conflict Resolution: Discovering Adaptive Behaviors for Young Black Men." Union Institute.

909. Stearns, R.P. (1974). "Factors Related to Fertility Values of Low-Income Urban Black Males: A Case Study." Case Western Reserve University.

910. Stevenson, H.C., Jr. (1985). "Generality and Social Validity of a Competency-Based Self-Control Intervention with Underachieving Students." Fuller Theological Seminary, School of Psychology.

911. Stolzenberg, R.M. (1973). "Occupational Differences in Wage Discrimination against Black Men: The Structure of Racial Differences in Men's Wage Returns to Schooling, 1960." University of Michigan.

912. Stovall, C.D. (1990). "Development of a Measure of White Counselor Racial Attitudes Toward Black Male Client Characteristics: The Counselor Situational Attitude Scale (CSAS)." University of Maryland College Park.

913. Sullivan, B.H., Jr. (1993). "Differential Aspects of Self-Esteem in the African-American Adolescent Male." University of South Carolina.

914. Summers, M.D. (1974). "Effects of Peer Behavior, Monetary Incentive, and Race of the Peer on Temporal Persistence in Fourth-Grade Black Males." Hofstra University.

915. Sweet, L.E. (1987). "Sexual Knowledge, Attitudes, and Behavior among Black Male Adolescents." University of Pennsylvania.

916. Taylor, S.C.F. (1992). "Pathways to Dropping Out." Virginia Polytechnic Institute and State University.

917. Thomas, J. (1990). "Black Male Character Types in Four Works by Alice Walker and Toni Morrison." Indiana University of Pennsylvania.

918. Thomas, M.M. (1996). "The African-American Male: Communication Gap Converts Justice into 'Just Us' System." University of Nevada, Reno.

919. Thomas, R.E. (1982). "Alcohol Abuse among Black Males in a Detoxification Center: A Study of Stress and Social Supports." Boston University Graduate School.

920. Thompson, S.H. (1993). "Adolescent Males' Body Image Perceptions of Themselves and Females." University of South Carolina.

921. Tiggs, K.S.D. (1995). "Exploring Philosophical Confusion as a Key Variable Regarding Violent Black-On-Black Crime: An Africentric Approach." Nova Southeastern University.

922. Tomlin, V.E. (1994). "A Mentor Program for Improving the Academic Attainment of Black Adolescent Males." University of Denver.

923. Towns, D.P. (1995). "The Impact of Structural Hypocrisy on the School Performance of Young African-American Males." American University.

924. Troy, K.A. (1992). "The Troy Leadership Academy." United Theological Seminary.

925. Van Etten, G.L. (1995). "Major Challenges, Coping Strategies and Support Systems Concerning Aids and Ethnicity." University of South Florida.

926. Wagner, C. (1993). "The Interactional Processes of Public Policies, Drug Treatment and Maturation Impacting on Black Male Ex-Offenders." University of Bridgeport.

927. Walia, K. (1979). "Locus-Of-Control Measures and Children's Academic Achievement within Black Father-Absent Families." Howard University.

928. Walker, J.T., Jr. (1990). "Relative Black Male Employment among Business Establishments: Relation to Management Orientation Toward Affirmative Action, Organizational Context, and Organizational Characteristics." University of Michigan.

929. Walker, P.W. (1983). "Sex-Role Stereotyping as a Factor Influencing Counselors' Advising of Black Male Students to Investigate Selected Allied Health Professions." Loyola University of Chicago.

930. Wallace, M.O. (1995). "Constructing the Black Masculine: Identity and Ideology in African-American Men's Literature and Culture." Duke University.

931. Ward, J.V.H. (1986). "A Study of Urban Adolescents' Thinking about Violence Following a Course on the Holocaust." Harvard University.

932. Weaver, G.D. (1989). "An Examination of Stress, Psychosocial Resources, and Physical Health among Older Black Men and Women." State University of New York at Stony Brook.

933. Wheeler, D.P. (1992). "Marginalization, Locus-Of-Control and Gender Identification: Mediating Variables in the Risk for Sexual Exposure to HIV among Young Urban Black Males." University of Pittsburgh.

934. White, L.S. (1986). "The Effect of Child Abuse and Neglect on Cognitive Development of Black Male Children." University of Illinois at Chicago.

935. Wiegman, R. (1988). "Negotiating the Masculine: Configurations of Race and Gender in American Culture." University of Washington.

936. Wiggins, C. (1993). "The Future for Blacks in America: The American Dream or a Pipe Dream?" Central Missouri State University.

937. Williams, J.L. (1989). "Factors That Contribute to the Achievement of Black Male Students at a Predominantly White University." University of Massachusetts.

938. Williams, R.F. (1987). "The Perceptions of Black Male Students Transferred into a Disciplinary Alternative School in Philadelphia." Temple University.

939. Williamson, B.L. (1980). "Retirement Issues: A Study of the Knowledge of Retirement and Retirement Planning among Elderly Black Males." California State University, Dominguez Hills.

940. Wilson, V.H. (1989). "The Measure of Manhood: The Fiction of Ernest J. Gaines." Tulane University.

941. Wingfield, R.P., Jr. (1995). "Factors Motivating Black Male Students to Pass the Virginia Literacy Passport Test after Failing Several Administrations and Being Labeled 'Ungraded.'" Virginia Polytechnic Institute and State University.

942. Wood, N.P., Jr. (1983). "Black Trust: Coping among Black Males." University of Maryland College Park.

943. Woodard, Q.E.(1984). "Effect of Father-Presence and Father-Absence on the Self-Concept of Black Males in Special Education and Regular Education Classes." Western Michigan University.

944. Woolfson, N.M. (1985). "Human Criteria in the Design of Hostels for Black Male Contract Employees." University of Pretoria.

945. Worley, C.G. (1990). "A Descriptive Study of the Factors Related to the Incidence of Alcoholism among Black Males in Metropolitan Detroit." Wayne State University.

946. Young, A.A., Jr. (1996). "Pathways, Possibilities, and Potential: Young Black Men and Their Conceptions of Future Life Chances." University of Chicago.

Conclusions

A better understanding of the African-American male in American life and thought depends to a very large measure on the quantity and quality of research and scholarship on this segment of the American population. This volume is only just the beginning of such an effort. As we examined close to 1000 sources on the African-American male in America, it is evident that the African-American male has been inextricably involved in practically all aspects of American life, good or bad. Our objective was two-fold: to determine the nature and the scope of scholarship on the African-American male, and to examine the extent to which scholarship has addressed the problems that confront the African-American male in our society. We believe that this compilation reflects meeting these objectives.

It is our hope that this book will stimulate further research, especially in the areas that require more attention. For example, there needs to be more applied research to demonstrate what works in solving the African-American male problems. Equally important are theory based demonstration research models for replication. Perhaps, most important, is the lack of any meaningful work on the research done by African-American males themselves. The absence of such a document represents a wide gap in any effort to create a better public understanding of the African-American male. Indeed a publication of this nature, that is, a selected compilation of scholarly works by African-American males would complement the present volume of selected annotated bibliography on African-American males.

If our scholars, researchers and practitioners at all levels of the American experience are to be capable of lifting us and moving us, they will have to believe in the people of this nation--a people so able to perform splendidly and so inclined to perform indifferently, so troubled in their efforts to find a future worthy of their past, so capable of greatness and so desperately in need of encouragement to achieve that greatness.   The African-American males themselves must continue to act against all odds if they believe strongly enough to reach for unreachable stars and dream of impossible victories and have at the same time the rational ingenuity to design their future and proper place in American life.

Author Index

Numbers are referring to entry numbers.

Abdul, Raoul, 021
Abron, J., 415
Aikens, C., 416
Akbar, N., 417
Akers, T.A., 632
Al Aswadu, A., 083
Alan-Williams, Gregory, 084
Aldridge, Delores P., 196
Allen, E., Jr., 418
Allen, M., 419
Allen, Robert L., 197, 208, 420
Allen, W.R., 421, 422
Als, H., 423
Alston, D.N., 424
Alston, Harvey, 143
Althouse, Ronald, 372
Amdur, Neil, 365
Anderson, E., 425
Anderson, Elijah, 198
Anderson, Jervis, 115
Anderson, M., 426
Andrews, William L., 199, 216, 263, 427

Aptheker, Herbert, 200, 201, 334
Asante, Molefi K., 428, 429
Ashe, Arthur, 364, 365, 366, 367, 430
Astor, Gerald, 368
Austin, Bobby, 144, 431
Austin, Lettie J., 001

Bahr, S.J., 557
Bair, Barbara, 238
Baker, Houston A., 002
Baker, William J., 369
Baker-Fletcher, Garth, 202
Balagoon, Kuwasi, 049
Bankes, James, 370
Baraka, Ras, 014
Barbeau, Arthur E., 203
Barker, Lucius Jefferson, 288, 289
Barnes, A.S., 432
Beatty, L.A., 151
Bedau, Hugh Adam, 086
Belk, S.S., 644
Bell, C.C., 433

Subject Index

Numbers are referring to entry numbers.

About the Compiler

JACOB U. GORDON is Professor of African and African American Studies and a Research Fellow at the University of Kansas, Lawrence, Kansas.

ISBN 0-313-30656-7

HARDCOVER BAR CODE